THIS BOOK IS FOR YOU IF...

- You think you might be in the wrong pond

- You think you might be worth more bread

- You are ready to soar, but don't know how

- You are fed up with ducking and diving

- You keep paddling, but are not getting anywhere

- You keep quacking, but no one is listening

- Nobody is throwing bread at you

- You are quacked out

- You are fed up with feathers being ruffled

- You are scared of being a lame duck

Are you plagued by constant negative dialogue running around in your head? Like the incessant quacking of a duck? Find out here how to *Shut The Duck Up!* for good!

WHAT OTHER DUCKS ARE SAYING...

A five star read!

"This book was so refreshing! So many other books take ages to get to the point, surrounding the key learning principle with lots of unnecessary waffle."

"Probably one of the best self-improvement books I have read in recent years. I hope other self-help masters follow your no-fluff approach to teaching....thank you!"

This book is a wonderful self-help read and can apply to all ages. I love the fact that it validates with real cases and events. It's authentic and logical. A useful tool that you can pick up and use at any time. It gives helpful and realistic ways to implement change and achieve individual goals. It's engaging and it just makes sense! Thank you, Pete and Bobby, for this little 'gem'."

"I have read this book over the weekend. It's clear and makes lots of sense. Lots of reference points too. I will be going back to refer to the points that are relevant to me right now. I am sure I will keep dipping into this book again and again. Definitely worth the money paid."

"Five stars for a GENIUS READ!!! This is a simple and yet captivating read that anyone and everyone can benefit from!"

"Simple, to the point and lacking all the pretentiousness of other similar, and massively more expensive offerings. A down-to-earth effective offering from a down-to-earth effective author and, it would seem, top bloke, who understands people. Written with a lot of passion from men who obviously took a lot from growing up and from experiences in college, family and tradition. For the money, it has to be on the shelf of all people who work in raising aspirations."

"Grabbed this book yesterday and, if I'm honest, thought it would be a heavy read; how wrong was I? It covers some amazing simple stuff in helping us shut up our own duck, and the free bonus video the authors give you is brilliant. Thank you for a great book; this will help a lot of people."

"We all get caught up in life and influences more than we realise, but this book will SET YOU FREE!!! LOVED IT!!!!"

BOBBY CAPPUCCIO

Bobby Cappuccio is an internationally recognised speaker and author. Bobby has assisted countless thousands of trainers, managers and industry leaders in the world's most well-known organisations to facilitate remarkable changes in their businesses.

Bobby is a co-founder of PTA Global, an international personal trainer education company. Formerly the director of professional development for the National Academy of Sports Medicine, Bobby has written articles for several fitness publications, been a contributing author of two textbooks, and has been a keynote speaker for leading industry conferences.

PETE COHEN

Pete Cohen is a life coach, public speaker, TV presenter and bestselling author of eleven books about making positive life changes and weight loss.

He works as a peak performance coach for world-class athletes, including Dame Ellen MacArthur, Ronnie O'Sullivan and Dame Sally Gunnell.

Pete is well known for his regular morning TV appearances on GMTV and BBC2's *Confidence Lab*. He was recognised internationally for defining the 'Formula for Happiness' in 2003. As a life coach, life strategist and human behaviourist, he works with people to create positive change in their lives.

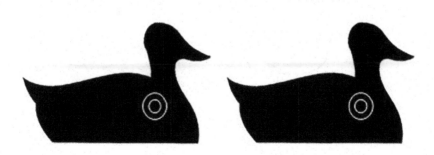

JOIN OUR POND!

Find out what's hatching by
joining our family!

Mi365 is a live broadcast every weekday at 7 a.m (UK time)
which is designed to help people make positive changes in
their lives. Thousands of people tune in live, or watch the
replay, to benefit from my free coaching.

Join me, Pete Cohen, and learn how I can help you to change
your mindset and improve the way you live your life:
https://mi365elite.me/free-group

It's eggciting!

DEDICATION

No matter how many other ducks there
are in your pond,

no matter who reaches the bread first,

no matter who has ruffled your feathers,

or led you to believe you are an ugly duckling,

I dedicate this book to you.

∼

We would like to thank Chris Day from Filament Publishing for bringing this project to life and adding his advice and expertise. We both really appreciate you, and look forward to sharing the success of this book with you.

don't quack like a duck, soar like an eagle.

ken blanchard

be like a duck. Calm on the surface,
but always paddling
like the dickens
underneath.

Michael Caine
(not a lot of people know this)

BOBBY CAPPUCCIO

PETE COHEN

Published by
Filament Publishing Ltd
16, Croydon Road, Waddon, Croydon,
Surrey, CR0 4PA, United Kingdom
Telephone +44 (0)20 8688 2598
www.filamentpublishing.com

'Shut the Duck Up'

© 2015 Bobby Cappuccio and Pete Cohen

ISBN 978-1-910819-40-1

Cartoon illustrations by Grizelda
www.grizelda.net

Printed by IngramSpark

Table of Contents

Whenever it all gets too much, you need to get some head space so that you can put your thoughts in order. Find somewhere peaceful - your bed, a park bench - and start filtering through the duck talk in your head. In emergencies, when you really can't get away from family or work colleagues, go and lock yourself in the loo for five minutes!

if it looks like a duck, and
quacks like a duck,
we have at least to consider
the possibility that we have
a small aquatic bird
of the family anatidae
on our hands.

douglas adams

Preface

Why 'Shut The Duck Up'?

You might be wondering why this book is called *Shut the Duck Up!* An old pal and colleague of mine worked at one time with a top, professional sportsman. On one occasion, the sportsman, who was well known for his difficult attitude, exploded in anger during a match and wound up attacking a spectator. It was my friend's job to help the athlete understand his actions and re-focus his energy. However, during their session, my pal could see it wasn't happening. The sportsman looked confused by all the talk of inner voices and dialogue. However, when asked about his 'self-talk', the light bulb suddenly went on in his head:

"Ah," he said. "You mean the duck in my head?"

The athlete equated the internal monologues of his mind with a duck that just kept 'quacking' away at him, telling him what to do and often intensifying his stress, worry and anger.

When my friend told me this story, it really resonated with me. I, like this sportsman and so many other people, also have a duck in my head. And just like the athlete, when my duck quacks, it's not necessarily a supportive, soothing stream of consciousness. It's frequently harsh and, even when it's trying to help, has often given me bad advice – don't try in case you fail, don't rise in case you fall, keep quiet, stay small, run away.

My duck began quacking at me when I was a child and was diagnosed with learning difficulties including attention deficit disorder (ADD) and dyslexia. Of course, I didn't understand what this really meant except that it made me feel different to others and 'not good enough' (that was the duck starting to talk).

QUAAAAACK!

The quacking only grew louder as I entered my teens and twenties. Getting accepted to study in a college was a struggle for me but, against the odds, I succeeded. However, even after I left college and become a personal trainer with regular television appearances on GMTV and BBC2's *Confidence Lab*, I still couldn't stop the negative quacking of my inner duck. Clients that I worked with would thank me for helping them turn their lives around or tell me how great I was, and I would openly accept their compliments while secretly not believing them to be true.

It was only when I reached my late thirties and my now-wife, Hannah, was diagnosed with an aggressive brain tumour and given 18 months to live, that I finally learned how to shut my own duck up. Faced with the choice of doing nothing and losing the woman I loved, or focusing my mind on overcoming my own fears to do whatever I could to get the right medical help for Hannah, I chose the latter.

My duck was telling me there was nothing I could do, that I shouldn't try and help because it wouldn't turn out well. I realised that this was, of course, the truth. Or, at least, this was the truth if

I continued to listen to my duck. But what if I focused my thoughts elsewhere? What if I focused my thoughts on being strong, on finding a solution, on the opposite of everything my duck was saying to me – what then?

I did this and I found a doctor in the States who was able to treat Hannah successfully. It wasn't an easy path. In fact, it challenged and terrified us both. Even to this day, five years later, when Hannah goes for a check-up and a scan, my duck starts its loud quacking. But now I know how to shut it up. I have the tools to stop the mindless chatter and the negative self-talk. And I want to pass those tools onto you.

My co-author and good friend, Bobby Cappuccio, began hearing his duck when he was only a child too. Born with a facial deformity, he was emotionally and physically abused by his adoptive mother's partner and lived his early life in constant fear for his safety. On his first day of school, when the other students and even the teachers looked at him with wary or taunting eyes, he heard the first soft quacking of his duck. The quacks told him that being born this way, that being adopted, that being a punchbag for his stepfather, all meant the same thing: that he was born bad.

The older he got, the worse his life became, which only served to build his duck's credibility. He developed facial tics, Tourette's Syndrome and Obsessive Compulsive Disorder.

However, along the way he began to meet people who saw something else in him. People who saw a spark; a little boy with hopes and dreams, just like any other little boy. In his late teens, he underwent two surgeries to 'correct' his facial defects and he began to listen to those people who were saying the opposite of what his duck was telling him. Little by little, Bobby realised that maybe his duck was actually wrong; maybe it was all quackery after all.

Over the years, Bobby has risen in the field of fitness management and personal development to become an internationally recognised and widely sought-after speaker and author. And now, like me, he is eager to share with you the insights and strategies he has spent his life seeking; to help you not only quiet the incessant quacking of your inner duck, but to enrich your life beyond what you now might think is possible.

Our beliefs, thoughts and emotions profoundly affect what we say to ourselves, the questions we ask ourselves, and therefore, the attitude we have toward any given situation in our lives. The perceptions we form in our inner world determine what actions we take (or fail to take) in our outer world.

So if we desire a different result in any area of our lives, we need to stop the duck quacking and create a different dialogue in our head. That's what this book is about. It's about helping you to identify where you are limiting yourself and giving you the simple steps to take your life to the next level. It's about empowering you to be accountable for your actions and therefore authentic in your inter-actions. In short, it's about turning the constant chatter of your mind into a steady and strong voice that questions, rather than quacks, and leads you to the life you want.

Pete Cohen

Introduction

So What's All This Quacking About?

Most of the quacking that you hear in your head is based on three widely held beliefs about change. These beliefs contribute to much of the struggle and frustration many people have in their lives - the wish to change their careers, to change their weight, or any aspect of their lives – and are highlighted throughout *Shut The Duck Up!*

Eliminate these myths, and you'll eliminate much of what has frustrated your efforts to make changes in multiple areas of your life so far.

These myths are:

Myth No.1: People don't like to change.

The research on this is clear: many of the factors essential to peak performances in multiple areas of our lives are intrinsic factors. The effectiveness to which we initiate or respond to change in our outer world is dependent on our inner world. Change, if it is to last, must be self-directed and have an element of autonomy. As Peter M. Senge said in his book, *The Fifth Discipline*, "People don't resist change, they resist being changed."

All of us have experienced people in our lives, whether friends, family, teachers who have either implicitly or explicitly expressed their expectations for our lives; what we should do with our life, work, relationships, who we should be with, and even who we should be. If we accept their expectations for our lives, we get their approval, if we don't, we fall into disfavour, or worse, rejection.

However, if we fulfil their expectations for our lives, we get more than their approval, we get to suffer as Henry David Thoreau put it, the "quiet desperation" of continually suppressing our creativity, individuality and passions to live out a script we didn't even write, just to be rewarded with conditional acceptance. Even if these people are well meaning, and they often are, this is a recipe for a life of frustration, discontent, perhaps even resentment. If we are forced or manipulated to conform our lives to the expectations of others, no matter what we achieve, fulfilment is fleeting at best.

Myth No.2: Experts are the authority on how to make changes in my life.

This makes sense intuitively; however, it's false. Edward Deci and Richard Ryan are the creators of Self-Determination Theory. This theory, which is widely accepted and respected in the field of psychology, asserts that change, if it is to last, must be intrinsically motivated. This means that we change for our own reasons. We don't change because it makes sense to someone else, or because an author presents a solid argument why we should. We don't change because a speaker gave a rousing motivational speech, or we were made to feel guilty into changing by people who think we should and have no problem 'shoulding' all over us. These experiences may create momentary emotional shifts that make us consider or even initiate change, but it's seldom enough to sustain it.

Myth No.3: Change is a long and hard process.

Often, change is neither long nor hard. The mental and emotional preparation for change is long and hard. The fear of judgement, rejection and failure in the face of change is hard. You cannot control the opinions of others. If the pursuit of an outcome that is worthwhile to you is met with judgement and rejection, you probably never had the full support and acceptance of that individual in the first place. Further, the setbacks you encounter along the way to achieving or becoming anything significant often are essential to helping you grow into the person who is capable of actualising the results you desire most.

The difference in how you respond to such situations is in the meaning you attach to them. In this book, you will learn how to bring about the changes you seek whilst experiencing reward in the process, not just the end result.

The research in behavioural change reveals that very rarely does change come as a result of total immersion. It is often a slow, non-linear process of single small steps culminating in a bountiful journey.

Taking this book, for example, just ten minutes a day, one key at a time, and then applying what you learn, can compound into life-altering changes before you know it. Transforming any meaningful aspect of your life is not a sprint, it's a marathon; and we will be there every step of the way.

How to Use This Book

Your brain is busy. Advertisers, friends, family, colleagues, and the TV all scream for its attention. It's bombarded with advice, judgement, criticism, condemnation, demands. Some of it is positive, some important, and much of it is irrelevant nonsense: collectively, it's draining and disconcerting. Add in your own duck, quacking away at you with every decision, intention or thought that you have, and it's no wonder it can all get a bit overwhelming.

Shut The Duck Up! offers you information based on cutting-edge research and over 60,000 hours of experience that we have amassed through years working with top athletes, industry leaders, senior management, and an array of other people from many walks of life.

We've used this expert knowledge to deliver purposeful instructions in 50 easy-to-digest guidelines or, as we call them, 'keys'. We know that you just might not have time to read this book from cover-to-cover, so we specifically designed it to allow you to dip in and out as you like. In this way, you can use the keys to unlock the insight you need to get focused without feeling the pressure to set aside a couple of hours each day to do so. They'll give you some clarity on what you want, and help you make that vision into your reality.

Remember, these guidelines are the product of our combined experience, expertise and conclusions, but you'll bring to your reading of them your own wisdom and wonder. Consider everything, then take what works for you and don't be scared - in fact, be determined - to question any loud quacking you start to hear as you read!

The 8 Golden Promises

Before we get going with the 50 key guidelines, let's first clarify what the flipside is of shutting the duck up. Doing this will enable you to see that even by dipping into this book for a few minutes each day, you are in fact paving a path to becoming a better, bolder, more confident you.

Every time we commit to changing an aspect of our lives, we are, in effect, making a promise to ourselves. By picking up this book, you've made the decision to drop the internal duck talk that's been preventing you from living the life you want. To keep to this commitment, we're asking you now to make a series of simple but far-reaching promises to yourself. We call these the '8 Golden Promises' and we encourage you to take them seriously. If you do, you'll find it easier to use this book to actually get results.

Promise #1: I Promise that I'll Strive to be an Eagle

You've probably heard the expression, "If it looks like a duck, swims like a duck and quacks like a duck, then it probably is a duck."

There's a certain type of person that we like to call 'ducks'. They go waddling through life, quacking on about their hardships.

There are also 'chickens'. These are people who know exactly what they want, but are too afraid to ever go and pursue it.

And then, there's the 'eagle'. Someone who recognises the challenges that they face, yet still manages to soar above them.

Ask yourself what sort of a person you are now. Is that who you'd like to be, or are you ready to ruffle some feathers and make a change? If you're currently a duck or a chicken, make the promise to yourself now that you're going to strive to be an eagle.

Promise #2: I Promise not to be a Sitting Duck

A chicken is content just scratching around his pen, living within the comfort of his confines. If the shadow of a hawk appears above the chicken, then it will run for cover, rather than facing the danger.

Many people are content where they are, simply because they've grown comfortable being there. Emerson said, "People wish to be settled; only as far as they are unsettled is there any hope for them." In other words, the only way to grow and position yourself as a master of change (rather than a victim of change) is to get comfortable being uncomfortable!

Change is vital if we're ever to grow. And change can be unsettling, sure. But people with the 'chicken' mindset are terrified of change; they'll metaphorically run for cover and hope it passes.

An eagle, however, will not accept boundaries. If a hawk appears, it won't hide from it, it'll pursue it. Life's winners are like the eagle; they don't want to be fenced in either. They desire to spread their wings, and fly is too strong for them to ignore.

Even though they may have been a 'chicken' in the past, something changed within them, and they wanted to be free. Eagles long to fly higher and higher. When a challenge appears that requires them to grow, they'll pursue it with relish because they understand that the situation is actually an opportunity to become better.

An eagle knows that in order to have more or do more, you must become more. Once you have seen the world from the perspective of an eagle, you can never go back to the chicken coop.

Promise #3: I Promise to be Eagle-Eyed

Eagles have an extraordinary ability to focus. Their eyes can focus on objects that are several miles away. Not only that, but an eagle is unique in having two sets of eyelids. They enable him to fly towards his destination without being blinded by distractions, even if he flies directly into the sun.

Life's winners consistently focus on their major purpose, irrespective of the distractions that tempt all of us. Goethe said, "Things that matter most must never be at the mercy of things that matter least"; winners live their lives by that premise.

Promise #4: I Promise to Fly with Birds of a Feather

Who do you surround yourself with? Ducks go waddling through life, quacking on about their hardships. They often seek out the company of other ducks, because they're comfortable being in a flock that quacks at them constantly, insisting that they give up their self-determination and just blend in with everyone else.

Eagles don't live in flocks; they mate for life. But if her mate dies, the female won't take up with just any other eagle. She puts any potential mate to the test. They'll fly together for a while, then she'll fly down to the ground, pick up a stick and fly up high into the air. Then, she'll loosen her talons and let the stick fall; he must pick up the stick before it hits the ground. If he doesn't, he's history, but it doesn't stop there. She'll get a bigger stick and go to the heights and then drop it. Again, he is expected to catch it. She will keep doing this until she is carrying small logs. Eventually, she'll pick up a stone, fly high and then drop it for him to catch.

There's a good reason for this behaviour; one day, they'll have eaglets, and they'll teach their babies to fly. If one of the eaglets runs into trouble and falls from the sky, she needs to know that he'll be able to catch it.

Who are the five people that you're closest too, and choose to surround yourself with? Eagles understand that you're a mirror of these people, so if you want to move past where you are now, be aware of your associations.

Ask yourself:

- Do the people around you support you and add to your quality of life? Or do they discourage you?
- If you fell, would they catch you until you could fly on your own? Or would they point out that you fell and offer you their opinions on why you couldn't make it?
- Can they 'fly' themselves? And if not, do they try to stop you from doing so?

An eagle doesn't bother with birds that don't want to fly high. If they nip at him, he will simply extend his wings and rise to heights that they'll never know.

Many of us are surrounded by people who've never had the courage to pursue their dreams, so they spend their lives trying to squash the ambitions of others.

Be careful what company you keep. Do you seek out people who keep you down, or who encourage you to fly?

Promise #5: I Promise to Feather My Nest...
But Not Too Much!

When an eaglet is a baby, it rests in a nest lined with feathers and rabbit fur, and simply eats, sleeps and squawks when it needs attention. But one day, the party's over. The mother comes to the nest and starts screaming, then she rips out the comfy lining from the nest, and tears up the sticks that make the nest.

The eaglet won't have a place to rest anymore; he won't be able to get comfortable, so he's forced to start learning to fly.

Are you so comfortable in a certain situation, that it's actually holding you back?

Promise #6: I Promise to Spread My Wings without Worry

Baby eagles would never learn to fly without encouragement from their parents. The mum and dad nudge their eaglets to the edge of the nest. They then take a morsel of the babies' favourite food to a tree branch, in full view of the starving eaglets, and make sounds to pretend that they're eating and enjoying the food.

The little birds start to focus on how much they want to eat, more than their fear of being so close to the edge. They want the food so badly that they start to scream; eventually, their hunger compels them to try flapping their wings. As they beat the air, they rise from the nest and then flap and scream their way onto the other limb. And once they've made that first flight, the world suddenly opens up for them.

If you have a hunger driving you, you must flap your wings and go out on a limb. You must go somewhere you've never been before, in order to achieve what you crave.

When your desire is great enough, your resolve will be strong enough to go from where you are now to where you want to be, regardless of the sacrifices needed. Desire drives all achievements, and will enable you to spread your wings without worry.

Promise #7: I Promise I'll Come Home to Roost

An eagle's eyes are miraculous. They contain a network of fine lymph tubes ('pectins') that contain electrolyte fluid. In a similar way to how a compass works, they're affected by the magnetic pull of the North Pole. The tubes are fluid when the eagles are young, but as they mature, they set in relation to the bird's place of birth. This means that when a mature eagle is away from his nesting ground, he has a sense of pressure and pain until he returns home.

When you have your true purpose, then it becomes your true destination, like the eagle's desire to return home. Your internal self will feel balanced and secure in this world where the external factors rapidly change.

If you stray from your values, and what is truly important to you, then you'll feel that intense pressure to return to what's right for you.

Promise #8: I Promise to Rise Above It

An eagle flies on the air currents. He folds his wings, he will drop. No matter what storms are raging, we must keep our wings spread so we can rise above it. Use your skills to avoid turbulence in your life; when you're always learning, then you'll be able to better deal with the wind when the storm comes. Commit to being better tomorrow than you are today, every day!

In the words of Lee Stoneking:

"As long as there has been bondage, man has sought freedom.

As long as there has been a heaven, man has sought to fly.

As long as there have been battles, man has sought to be fearless.

As long as there have been obstacles, man has sought to subdue them."

Be an eagle, and soar above the storms in your life. Each storm is different. Each bout of turbulence will teach you something new, and enable you to better cope with the next disaster.

～

Key No. 1: Get Your Ducks in a Row

Whenever it all gets too much, you need to get some head-space so that you can put your thoughts in order. Find somewhere peaceful - your bed, a park bench - and start filtering through the duck talk in your head. In emergencies, when you really can't get away from family or work colleagues, go and lock yourself in the loo for five minutes!

When you're alone, take some deep breaths and then start to pick through the thoughts quacking inside your head. Examine all the messages and voices, and discard anything that doesn't resonate with you. Keep only the useful, meaningful thoughts. Wait until you are calm before you leave your refuge.

Give yourself the space to explore, clear and calm your thoughts when they overwhelm you.

"...I've brought myself, by long meditation, to the conviction that a human being with a subtle purpose must accomplish it, and that nothing can resist a will that will stake even existence upon its fulfilment."
- Benjamin Disraeli

Key No.2: Find Your Purpose and Then You'll Soar

Great achievement begins with a great purpose. Most individuals dream, wish and hope to get more out of life. Sadly, most of them will never achieve it, because they'll never step out in pursuit of that dream. They're too scared to go for what they want, as success isn't guaranteed.

They're worried that if they try, they might fail. Obviously, this behaviour makes no sense at all. If you don't go for what you want, then the only thing you'll get is a failure, as you're guaranteeing yourself a life full of disappointment and regret.

It's not enough to want things in your life to change. You have to change too. Once you've realised that, you've already begun to change. Certain situations in your life may never get easier, but you can get better at dealing with them.

So, what's meaningful to you? What's so meaningful that you're going to devote your life to its fulfilment? It actually doesn't matter what your chosen purpose is. As soon as you have one, you become great. Unfortunately, most people never get there. They never decide what their life is about. They simply pass the time, paying the bills, getting up and going to bed, without ever finding meaning in their lives.

Why do you exist? Grab a pen and some paper, and spend some time writing down the purpose of your life. If you are not absolutely clear yet, just write down the first thing that occurs to you, however, silly it may be. Then think about why that thought popped into your head, and how it connects to something important to you.

Let's write your mission statement. A declaration that answers the question, "Why do I exist?" Find the guiding principles behind everything you do, rather than a specific achievement. For example, "I am going to raise £1,000 for cancer research," is a fine intention, but not a mission statement. "I aim to be a charitable person," is a mission statement.

You can change your mission statement at any point in the future, but for now, write it as though will never change. You can include as many items as you like, so be sure to include everything that's important to you. Write a mission statement now, and start living by it today.

A sense of purpose gives you drive and direction in life. Be inspired by this story about the painter, sculptor, engineer, and architect Michelangelo. He was commissioned to sculpt the statue of David, a project that had already been started by other artists, but abandoned. None of the others had been able to work with the supplied block of marble, as its grain made it extremely difficult to work with.

When Michelangelo saw the marble, he visualised "The David" trapped inside. For years, he worked relentlessly, chiseling away at the marble, and refining the sculpture.

When the piece was finally complete, it was unveiled to a crowd who was astonished at its magnificence. When asked how he was able to create such a masterpiece with the same marble that other notable sculptors struggled with, Michelangelo explained, "I saw an angel in the stone and carved until I set him free."

Michelangelo knew his purpose, and had a clear vision of David in his mind before it existed in reality. He was willing to work continuously, every day, for years, to bring that vision from his mind into being.

If you are committed to your purpose, clear about your vision, and willing to do what is necessary to make it real, then you will never have to wish for the life you desire. That's because you will achieve the life you desire, sculpt your world as you want it to be, and become the masterpiece you deserve to be.

if you keep your feathers well oiled,
the water of criticism will run off
as from a duck's back.

ellen Swallow richards

Key No.3: Dream Big, Fly High

W e've both always been big daydreamers. As a result, we used to get told off at school for daydreaming in class. Bobby has a particularly lasting memory of his English teacher – probably trying to be helpful in her own way – telling him, "Dreamers don't go anywhere in life."

Shortly after she told him this, he saw a TV programme about the life of Dr. Martin Luther King Jr, the American Civil Rights Activist. He was mesmerised as he watched Dr. King deliver his famous "I Have a Dream" speech. Here was a man with a clear vision, who used his eloquence and passion to share his dream with millions of people. He made it seem so real. Bobby remembers feeling as though the world-famous activist and Nobel Peace Prize winner put his vision directly into his heart and mind. "And so, even though we face the difficulties of today and tomorrow, I still have a dream. [..] I have a dream that my four little children will one day live in a nation where they will not be judged by the colour of their skin, but by the content of their character."

Dr. Martin Luther King Jr's dream became a reality 45 years after he made his historic speech, when Barack Obama was sworn in as the 44th President of the United States, the first African American to hold the title.

Great people have great visions, and those visions become reality. You might have visited Disney World, and its fantastic Epcot theme park. Epcot's name came from the acronym 'Experimental Prototype Community of Tomorrow,' and was Walt Disney's vision of a utopian city.

In his own words: "EPCOT... will take its cue from the new ideas and new technologies that are now emerging from the creative centres of American industry. It will be a community of tomorrow that will never be completed, but will always be introducing and testing and demonstrating new materials and systems. And EPCOT will always be a showcase to the world for the ingenuity and imagination of American free enterprise."

Unfortunately, after Disney's death in 1966, the construction of Epcot was postponed until the late 1970s. It finally opened in 1982 with a lavish ceremony, including – fittingly – the song *We've Just Begun to Dream*.

The park is still tremendously popular to this day, and people come from all over the world to experience its magic. It's been told that a reporter once remarked to Walt Disney's brother, Roy, that "it's too bad Walt didn't live to see this." Roy sharply corrected him with the reply, "Walt saw it first, and that's why you're seeing it now."

The bigger our dreams, the deeper our desire. Our lives will only change when we ourselves change; and we only have the impetus to start changing when our reasons exceed our excuses.

Anais Nin summed it up beautifully: "The day came when the risk to remain tight in a bud was more painful than the risk it took to blossom." We want to help you start blossoming, and to realise your dream!

Unfortunately, you'll still come across people, like Bobby's English teacher, who'll criticise you for daring to dream that you can fly high. We feel sorry for these people, because they don't have the imagination or drive to follow (or even have!) their own dream. Instead, we follow the advice of the author, philosopher and transcendentalist Henry David Thoreau. He said, "If you have built your castles in the air, your work need not be lost; that is where they should be. Now put foundations under them."

What's your dream? When you have a dream that's big and clear enough, then you'll get the courage to start making it happen.

Key No.4: Make It Real, Write It Down

We've already spoken about the importance of mission statements, and now we'd like you to record your goals too. Bobby still remembers the first time he decided to concentrate on what he really wanted to achieve with his life. He had just read about a 20-year study that was conducted by Yale University from 1953-1973. So it goes, back in 1953, the entire graduating class of Yale was asked if they had clearly defined, written goals for their lives once they left university. Surprisingly, out of the entire graduating class of Yale, only 3% of them had clearly defined written goals and plans for their achievement!

In 1973, Yale interviewed the surviving members of the class of 1953 and discovered that the 3% that had clearly defined goals, and a written plan for their achievement, were earning more than the 97% that didn't... combined!

He was so inspired that he drove straight to the shops, bought a notebook and a brand new pen, and then hurried to a café where he found a quiet table. He sat there for the next few hours writing out all his long and short-term goals. What a powerful tool; he got so much insight out of doing that simple exercise.

Soon after, Bobby came across an article written in the December 1996 edition of *Fast Company Magazine*. Writer Lawrence Tabak uncovered both the Yale and another similar study, reported to have been conducted by Harvard, to be nothing more than an urban legend! He remembers the sinking feeling in his chest as a read the words of Fast Company research associate Beverly Waters, "we are quite confident that the 'study' did not take place. We suspect it is a myth."

He was a bit deflated until he realised that six months after he wrote his goals down, he took stock of his progress. He'd already achieved two of his most important goals and was well on the way to completing the third. More importantly, he realised that he was actually happier than he'd ever been. When he wrote down his goals six months earlier, he took action thereby giving himself a reputation to live up to. He unwittingly used cognitive dissonance to his advantage. He changed as a person.

You can get extraordinary results when you know what you want, write it down, make a plan, and then take consistent action until your plan becomes a reality.

Key No.5: It's Fine to Change Your Mind

What beliefs have you always held? And how closely have you ever examined them? We all carry beliefs around with us, but who knows how much of what we take for granted is actually correct?

Don't forget, for a long time, people believed that the world was flat. Anyone who dared to disagree often faced punishment, even death. And what about the belief that the Earth was the centre of the solar system, and was orbited by the sun? The astronomer Copernicus disproved this, but was so frightened of the possible repercussions that he didn't allow his works to be published until after his death. Galileo's findings on the same matter even cost him his freedom. He spent his last days under house arrest.

There's no way to know for sure if many of your beliefs are fact or fiction. So rather than asking yourself if a belief is true or false, try asking yourself, "Is this constructive or destructive?" If your belief is constructive and will help you live a better life and achieve your goals, then that's great. If your belief is destructive, it will probably be holding you back; so challenge it, re-write it and, if necessary, trash it completely!

When we make decisions and form our beliefs, we do it in good faith using the knowledge we have. However, we often realise much later that the information we had when making those decisions was incomplete. Never be scared to revise your beliefs and make changes as appropriate. Maybe that means letting go of something that once seemed incredibly important to you, but you must be prepared to keep learning as you go.

being born in a duck yard
does not matter,
if only you are hatched
from a swan's egg.

hans Christian andersen

Key No.6: Know Your Needs

As humans, we all have needs that unite us, drive us, and explain our behaviour and beliefs. The American psychology professor, Abraham Maslow, summed these up in his 1943 work 'A Hierarchy of Needs'. These needs are grouped from the most fundamental (at the bottom) to the need to fulfil our potential (at the top).

So, if you look at the bottom layer, you'll see the 'physiological needs'. These are the most basic human needs of all: breathing, food, water and sleep. Without these, we cannot function properly.

Above that are our 'safety needs', such as being secure within our employment, our family, and health and home. I'm sure you've experienced how horribly unsettling life can be when anything is disturbed in this category. For example, losing your job, moving house, or when someone you love is ill.

The layer above that addresses our need to feel loved and to belong. That can be in our relationships with our friends, within our family, and having a bond of physical intimacy with our partner.

Further up the pyramid are our esteem needs. It's important that we have a sense of self-esteem and self-confidence, that we feel respected by others, and that we in turn respect others.

Towards the top is our desire to fully achieve our potential or 'self-actualisation' (as Maslow puts it). There are many different ways that this could be expressed. For example, it could be expressed by a desire to think and act creatively, to be spontaneous, to solve problems, and to approach life without prejudice.

Each person will experience this differently. One person might choose to express their self-actualisation through painting, another by becoming a fine cook, another by being a good parent, another by spending time getting to peak fitness.

Crowning the pyramid is 'self-transcendence'. This is the need to contribute to something beyond ourselves, and the ability to see the world from a universal perspective.

So, how do these needs explain our behaviour? Well, there are always reasons behind what we do. Whether consciously or subconsciously, everything we do meets one of our needs. So if we don't like our behaviour - or the results that it produces - then it's time to examine it closely.

We often gloss over our actions. Take, for example, a dieter who starts a new diet, full of good intentions, but then binges on chocolate the next day, and moans, "I've just not got any willpower!" That's neither helpful, nor accurate. What if a particular behaviour pattern sabotages one need, but fulfils another need?

Our dieter does want to eat healthily (to self-actualise), and though binge-eating chocolate sabotages her goal of self-actualisation, it actually achieves another goal. Binge-eating distracts her from the problems that she's having with her husband, for example, thus giving her a false sense of security.

In this case, our dieter doesn't actually need chocolate. What she needs is to express her fears to her husband, to work through her issues with him until they are resolved and she feels reassured. If she can't look within herself and realise what she actually needs, that unfulfilled need will continue to perpetuate the behaviour. A pattern will develop and become reinforced until it turns into an established habit and becomes harder and harder to break: she gets stressed, so she eats.

It's wrong to explain our behaviour with negative language; "I'm lazy!" "I'm weak!" "I can't change!" when actually, our behaviour is driven by our deep need for acceptance and emotional safety.

Do you secretly fear that if you don't put other people's needs before your own, they may withhold their approval of you? Many people have a mental model of conditional love, so to them loss of approval can feel the same as the loss of love. It doesn't matter how fit we are, what our job title is, how much we earn; if we don't feel loved, we're unlikely to feel safe and that's a fundamental human need.

We often get clients coming to us for help because they've repeatedly failed to achieve their fitness goals. After talking to them and enabling them to examine their behaviour, they come to understand that their current behaviour and staying unfit is actually 'beneficial'.

One particular client, who always puts other people's needs before her own, was subconsciously using this trait to sabotage her own weight loss attempts. Her attempts to do something for herself were always thwarted by other priorities and people that demanded her attention. So, by making herself indispensable to other people, she was able to feel significant and able to tell herself that because other people needed her so much, she is prevented from spending time on herself and therefore losing weight. Her desire to self-actualise was actually outweighed by her desire to feel loved, and therefore stopped her feeling sad that she hadn't reached her fitness goals. What looks like self-sabotage actually affords a person a measure of safety. So begins a cycle that's destined to repeat over and over and over again.

In my experience, I have found that emotional management is often as critical as weight management in getting a client to their goals!

So, start examining your own behaviour closely, and scrutinising the reasons behind it. What behaviour don't you like? What possible benefit could there be in your acting that way? Because there will be some sort of benefit there, even if it seems completely irrational at first glance.

behaviour arises from
the level of
one's consciousness.

Maharishi Mahesh Yogi

When you find a gap between your stated goals and your behaviour, ask yourself:

- What's stopping you from having what you want?
- What one behaviour is the greatest/most consistent obstacle to you reaching your goals?
- Why do you believe you keep repeating this behaviour?
- What need does this behaviour fulfil in you, and how do you know that's true?
- Who would you be without this behaviour?
- What other way could you fill that need? What would you need to know and do?
- What needs does this behaviour deprive you of?
- When you reach your goal, what needs will that achievement help you to fulfil?

How would you imagine the best version of yourself to be? And why? We're often surprised when our clients discuss their goals with us. It doesn't matter what their goals are (losing weight, increasing their fitness or improving their personal performance); what intrigues us is when we ask them why they want to achieve it. More often than not, they struggle to answer the question.

As with anything we do, if we're not clear about why we're doing it, we can feel disappointed when we achieve it, because, maybe, our goal was always something else entirely. For example, someone blames their current misery on their weight and convinces themselves that they'll feel happy if they could only lose a couple of pounds.

When they lose the weight, they're dismayed that their lives haven't magically improved, and that's because they hadn't properly examined the causes of their unhappiness.

If achieving a goal leaves us unsatisfied, this can be hugely demotivating. This unwelcome surprise can lead to enough upset and discouragement that we stop pursuing our other goals.

When you understand what needs your behaviour answers, you will start to understand what you really need. It's much easier to change your behaviour once you understand it.

discipline is the bridge
between goals
and accomplishment.

jim rohn

Key No.7: Mind the Gap

One night, as Pete travelled on the London Underground, he was snapped out of a daydream by the familiar announcement to "mind the gap" between the train and the platform. He must have heard that voice thousands of times, but he'd never actually thought about it properly before.

Was it really just a polite reminder to be careful as you stepped off the train? He began to see a profound significance in that little statement. Maybe it didn't just refer to the gap between the train and the platform. He could see it referring to the gap between who we are and who we are ultimately capable of being. Between where we are in our lives, and where we truly desire to be.

Once we decide on the meaning of our lives and the values that will guide us, how do we then act on the distance between where we are and where we want to be? How can we bridge the gap between who we are and who we ultimately desire to become?

Admiral James Stockdale was the Vice-Presidential running mate for Ross Perot in the 1992 United States Presidential Election. He was the highest-ranking military officer to be held prisoner at the 'Hanoi Hilton' during the Vietnam War, and was tortured 20 times during his imprisonment from 1965 to 1973. His autobiography, *Love and War*, contains explicit accounts of the brutality that he and the POWs endured.

In his highly acclaimed book, *Good to Great*, author Jim Collins recalls a conversation he had with Admiral James Stockdale. Collins asked him how he was able to cope with the physical, psychological and emotional stress of torture, not to mention the constant distress that came from not knowing whether each day would be their last.

Stockdale replied, "I never doubted not only that I would get out, but also that I would prevail in the end and turn the experience into the defining event of my life which, in retrospect, I would not trade."

Then Collins asked him, "Who didn't make it out?" to which Stockdale answered, "Oh, that's easy. The optimists." At this point in the conversation, Collins was completely confused. How could Stockdale claim that his faith was the reason he prevailed, but then say that optimism was a reason that some of his fellow Prisoners of War fell to the brutality of their captivity and never saw home again?

As Stockdale explained: "They were the ones who said, 'We're going to be out by Christmas.' And Christmas would come, and Christmas would go. Then they'd say, 'We're going to be out by Easter.' And Easter would come, and Easter would go. And then Thanksgiving, and then it would be Christmas again. And they died of a broken heart."

He then added, "This is a very important lesson. You must never confuse faith that you will prevail in the end - which you can never afford to lose - with the discipline to confront the most brutal facts of your current reality, whatever they might be."

Collins went on to describe this seemingly conflicted philosophy as "The Stockdale Paradox". It's a brilliant insight. If we take the metaphor that life is a journey, then regardless of the inevitable challenges we all face, some people will arrive at the destination of their choosing, while so many others will get lost along the way.

To successfully navigate any journey, you need a map. A map enables us to pinpoint exactly where we want to go, and crucially it also lets us figure out where we currently are. Armed with those two pieces of knowledge, it then lets us work out exactly how we're going to get to our destination. A map will help you identify the gap between where (or who) you want to be and where (or who) you actually are.

It's crucial to know the exact distance between your current reality and your desired reality. Starting to move from one to the other is a huge undertaking. If you're unclear or unwilling to "confront the most brutal facts of your reality," you might not be prepared for the sacrifices and detours you'll face along the way.

The question we all need to ask is "Why?" As the philosopher Friedrich Nietzsche said, "When man has a strong enough 'why,' he can bear any 'how.'"

Now, determine where you currently are on your map so you know exactly where you're starting from. What strengths and weaknesses do you have? They're the qualities that have brought you to where you are today in life.

So, ask yourself:

- What is the one skill or talent that has most contributed to the success that I have experienced in my life so far?
- Where do I lack confidence? Is it in certain social situations, or in certain areas of my life?
- What areas of my character need more work?
- What motivates me most of all?
- What part of my life makes me feel unhappiest?
- Which of my habits or traits are holding me back?

Doing the exercises above will determine where you are right now, and where you wish to go. The next step is to plan the route that you'll follow on your journey; the gap that you'll be bridging between your current reality and your future vision. Be prepared for the detours and roadblocks that you'll almost certainly encounter. A map can only show you the route, but it doesn't show you the obstacles or traffic that awaits you!

What you need to do now is to act as your own GPS. When you're out driving and you need to take an alternative route, your car's GPS doesn't get discouraged or disheartened, it simply programs a new route for you to follow. There's no single path to any destination; life is a series of calculations and re-evaluations. The key is to know where you want to go, to keep moving towards that goal, and to keep adjusting and tweaking your route as necessary.

You might even find that you learn more from the sometimes exasperating detours, than from the unobstructed open road. As the writer and cartoonist, Frank A. Clark said, "If you find a path with no obstacles, it probably doesn't lead anywhere."

So, when you plan your route, ask yourself:

- If I mastered one or two new skills, which ones would have the most positive and enduring effect on my work and my life?
- What are the three things that I must do daily in order to develop those skills? (For example, getting up early, studying for an hour a day, listening to audio programmes on your commute)
- What one goal would I most like to achieve this year? Why?
- What action can I take immediately as my first step on my journey?
- As I pursue my goal, what are the two or three things that could go wrong?
- What are two or three actions that I could take in response, if that should occur?

Finally, be prepared to discover that maybe joy and fulfilment don't lie purely at your destination, but also in who you'll become as you make your journey.

It's much easier to "retain the faith that you will prevail in the end, regardless of the difficulties" when you've already examined the potential problems and conflicts that you might face. The road to failure and disappointment is paved with blind optimism. Anything worth having has price, and if we know the price, we can decide whether or not we have the commitment to pay it.

Show me someone who
has done something worthwhile,
and i'll show you
someone who has
overcome adversity.

Lou holtz

Key No.8: Flying Through Time

Where do you actually live? We all exist in the present, but some people live in the past. They can't stop thinking about things that have gone wrong before. They retreat from life because they're scared of getting hurt again. Others live in the past, but it's not necessarily a negative thing. They interpret past events as lessons that will help them to do more, have more, and be more in the future.

There are other people who effectively live in the future. They can only think of what lies ahead, wanting the future where they have a bigger house and a better job. They're ultimately wishing their lives away, unable to appreciate what they have right now and incapable of learning from the past because they refuse to think about it. If you only look forward, you'll never see what's actually around you.

Those people who live in the present don't necessarily have it sorted either! Some people are hedonists; they're so immersed in the pleasures of today that they often fail to see the possibilities of tomorrow.

Dr. Phil Zimbardo of Stanford University has a theory on what he calls 'Time Perspective'. It's the study of where we chose to live (the past, the present or the future) and of what meaning we attach to each time zone.

Dr. Zimbardo asserts that those of us who are happiest, and who ultimately achieve their goals, are those who have a positive perspective on the past, are present minded enough to have a moderate degree of hedonism (but still retain their self-determination), and optimistic enough to have good expectations for the future.

Ideally, we need to have our eyes on the future, while our feet are firmly planted in the present. We need to have a goal to work towards, while enjoying the journey towards it. Here are some tips to achieve that mindset:

1. Set yourself clear daily goals. It makes your progress easy to measure, manage, and get motivated about.

2. Celebrate your achievements. Praise yourself! Congratulate yourself on weekly or even daily milestones, and remind yourself that every day takes you one step closer to your long-term ambitions.

3. Use the carrot, not the stick. You rarely need encouragement to go on holiday or out for a meal, because you know you'll enjoy yourself. The more pleasure we associate with an activity, the more likely we are to stick with it. Don't force yourself into an exercise routine or diet plan that you're not going to enjoy; it'll be nearly impossible to stick to.

Enjoy the present, and remember to learn from the past and look forward to the rest of your wonderful life!

∾

Key No.9: Don't Like The Result? Change the Cause

The philosopher Socrates taught that every effect or consequence in our lives is linked to a specific cause. This is known as 'The Socratic Law of Causality'.

Take the example of an unfaithful husband whose wife treats him with contempt, and doesn't trust him. What's the cause of his wife's behaviour? Some might say it's her temperament, or an issue with the whole concept of marriages, but obviously, it's neither of those things. The cause is his infidelity. It was his choice to be unfaithful, so he has to live with the consequence (i.e. a furious spouse).

Consequences don't only happen as a result of our conscious actions, they're a result of our subconscious actions too. So make sure that you're absolutely clear about who you want to be and what you want to do in life, and focus your energies on acting consistently towards your goals.

Let's say your lifelong dream is to open a coffee shop. However, while you daydream about that, in your 'real life', you have a job in an office, where you're working hard to get a promotion.

What will getting a promotion actually do for you? Will it get you any closer to your long-term goal of opening that coffee shop? In some senses, it will, because it will enable you to save more capital to finance your dream. In another sense, it might take you further away from your ambition! With the promotion will come a greater feeling of responsibility and commitment to your present job. You will spend more and more time at work, and feel less and less able to leave. The promotion will be the cause of several consequences. Ask yourself how you will feel a year after the promotion. Will you be delighted in your new status and sense of achievement? Or devastated because you've spent another year in your old job, and not running that coffee shop?

Make sure your short-term goals don't detract from your long-term goals. If you don't like the effects you're experiencing, you need to identify and change their causes; you might need to change yourself as well!

Key No.10: Stop Swimming in Circles

In our experience, we've found my clients are happiest when they're productive, fully engaged in life, and absolutely clear about what they want to achieve. Have you ever achieved something and, instead of feeling triumphant, had a hollow kind of feeling instead? It'll be because the achievement was wrong for you, and rather than moving you towards what you really wanted, it left you swimming in circles.

Here are five steps that we both use to help our clients determine what outcomes they really want, and how to swim towards them:

Clarity: You can't work on 'how' to achieve something until you've clearly established 'why' you want it. Your 'how' and 'why' must be aligned, otherwise you won't have the passion to stay the course and to try your best. Look at your goals, and start asking yourself why you want to achieve them. Are they really things you want to do, or things that other people have told you to do?

Action: Break down your goals. Look at the steps you need to fulfil in order to reach your goal.

For example, if you wanted to move house, you would need to prepare your existing house for a sale, and find a new house to live in. Write down three tasks that you can do every day, activities that are in line with your purpose, and move yourself closer to the life you desire and deserve. In our house example, every day you might clear out a cupboard, fix something that's broken in your existing house, and register with a new estate agent to try to find your dream house. You can break down any ambition into tasks.

Sensory Acuity: Is your strategy working? You need to determine whether or not the results you're actually getting are in line with what you actually want. Take stock of what's actually happened since you chose your goals. Have you moved any closer to your ambition?

Behavioural Flexibility: When the results you're getting don't match what you actually want, what then? Are you ready and willing to change your methods to change your results? Always have a Plan B, a Plan C, and even a Plan D, that you can switch to immediately!

Expectations of Self: What exactly do you expect of yourself? What would happen if you expected more from yourself in each situation than anyone else could expect from you?

The legendary conductor Benjamin Zander spoke wisely of expectations when he said: "I accept as a minimum criterion the maximum capacity that people have; I consider myself to be a relentless architect of the possibilities of human beings." Look at where you are, where you want to be and where you started from. Think about your journey; maybe it's time to choose a new destination.

Key No.11: Accept No Limitations

Patrick Henry Hughes was born on March 10, 1988. By the age of two, he already showed signs of extraordinary potential on the piano. As he grew, so did his talent and his passion for music. When he was 18, he joined the University of Louisville marching band; he played the trumpet and quickly became as much of an attraction as the games themselves.

Patrick drew huge crowds and media attention with his beautiful performances. He was soon invited to play the piano and sing at some of the legendary Grand Ole Opry concerts in Tennessee, alongside such country legends as Bryan White, Lonestar and Faith Hill.

As well as writing a book, Patrick has earnt many distinctions in his life, such as:

- The VSA (Very Special Arts) Panasonic Young Soloist International Winner
- The VSA Kentucky Young Soloist Award (five times!)
- Two-time Breaking Barriers Spotlight Award
- The Disney Wide World of Sports Spirit Award

We don't know if Patrick was born with his numerous talents, and his passion for music, or if he acquired them. However, we do know what he was born without: Patrick has a rare medical condition meaning that he was born without eyes.

He's never seen any of the games that he played trumpet for. He's never seen the stadiums he helped to fill. He's never seen the adoring audiences that come to support him.

When Patrick was born, his parents Patrick John and Patricia Hughes were devastated by his disabilities. Yet they quickly recognised their son's many talents and helped him to achieve his visions. As well as being born without eyes, he was born crippled. His father would push his wheelchair so he could 'march' with the marching band.

When asked to describe his disabilities, Patrick says "[they're] not disabilities at all but abilities. [...] God made me blind and unable to walk. Big deal! He gave me the ability... the musical gifts I have... the great opportunity to meet new people."

Patrick Henry Hughes knew the reality of his situation, accepted it, and then saw beyond it and dreamt of what could be possible. He's an inspiration.

Next time you tell yourself "I can't do that!" ask yourself whether that's a genuine limitation, or just an excuse.

~

Key No.12: Passion Gives You Energy

Some people are more than happy to give up a lot of themselves in the name of excellence, while others seem quite grudging to develop themselves. A friend worked as a trainer for prestigious organisations, including the BBC and Channel 4. When she started each course, she'd ask each attendee what they hoped to get out of each session. She was struck by the number of people who'd resentfully tell her that they actually didn't want to be there at all. Why were they spending so much of their lives doing something they weren't passionate about?

There seems to be some received wisdom that 'discipline' is the key to excellent, but that's not the whole story. In his book, *Nobodies to Somebodies*, author Peter Han interviewed 100 of the most highly accomplished people across various societies, including actors, company presidents, politicians and scientists.

Han determined that there was a magic ingredient for success present in everyone he interviewed. It wasn't just a burning intensity, but also the power to translate that into action. Everyone he spoke to had an energy that came from their huge passion for what they did.

These findings were echoed in *Fast Company Magazine's* feature in June 2010 on The 100 Most Creative People in Business. The issue highlighted the impressive achievements of figures as diverse as the late great Steve Jobs of Apple, Jamie Oliver and Lady Gaga.

These are people that tap the depths of their creativity, inspire everyone around them, strive for excellence, and continually reinvent themselves. Is it really discipline that allows them to do that? It's more than that. They've chosen a career for themselves doing something that they absolutely love. They're passionate about what they create. For them, the process of creation is as rewarding as the end result.

So, when you have an opportunity to learn, how should you approach it? If you go on a course thinking only about the outcome from the course, you could miss out on the pleasure of learning for its own sake.

We've spent time working with leaders from various industries, and we've noticed that they all devote time to improving their skills. Many outsiders would find this completely laborious (as our friend, the IT trainer, discovered). So, why do these leaders make themselves do it? The answer that comes back, time and time again, is, "Because I enjoy it."

We see it at networking events, at trade shows, at seminars: professionals who are passionate about learning. Their attitude isn't resentful. They don't feel that they have to be there, they're actually just happy that they get to be there. They seem to have more energy, passion and, crucially, more opportunity than the majority.

Try and identify what you love, and make it part of your life and your work. You don't have to strive to be Steve Jobs; it's simply about what makes you happy.

If you think you've lost your drive, take the time to recapture what you really want. If you define your dream, you will regain the passion to achieve it.

when you're surrounded

by people who share

a passionate commitment

around a common purpose,

anything is possible.

howard Schultz

Key No.13: It's What You Can Do, Not What You Can't Do, That Matters

Parents often tell their kids, "You can do anything or be anyone that you want to!" Whilst it's critical to encourage our children to fulfil their potential, it's also important not to give them unrealistic expectations. We can't do or be everything we want!

Itzhak Perlman is regarded as one of the world's finest violinists, yet he was stricken with polio at the age of four, which ravaged his legs. He'll never be a footballing hero, no matter how inspired he'd be by someone like David Beckham. Likewise, David Beckham, while certainly a world-class footballer, would probably never be able to play a violin as well as Perlman can, however much he wanted to.

Yet each of us has traits and skills that give us extraordinary potential in something. You are the only person who's ever been born with your distinctive mix of talents, experiences, disposition and desires. We are all truly extraordinary in some aspect.

When Pete was a child, he was told that he had a below-average IQ. He struggled with many daily tasks that most people take for granted, and worried that although he had the desire to achieve and the will to act, he might not possess the aptitude. You can imagine just how much quacking his duck was doing!

However, as he grew, he discovered he had a great talent for communicating, and for helping others to achieve their potential.

We all have our strengths and our weaknesses. Unfortunately, many of us, throughout our lives, have been criticised for our weaknesses, rather than praised for our strengths. This can lead to us eventually forgetting what our strengths are! Focus on your abilities. Use your unique talents and fulfil your potential.

Once you discover what you can do, what you can't do won't hold that much importance for you anymore.

～

Key No.14: Get Your Duck on Your Side

Most people underestimate themselves. Do you? Maybe you believe something about yourself that isn't just false, but is also damaging. Here's a typical false belief from someone struggling to lose weight: "I'm just a naturally fat person; I can't exercise, and I'm just too lazy."

Do you punish yourself like that? Ask yourself whether your beliefs are destructive or not. Dr. Martin Seligman has done much research into what he calls our 'explanatory style'. For example, after making a mistake, a person with destructive beliefs might say, "I'm so stupid, I always do that!" Now, that's a pretty harsh statement. It's personal ("I'm", "I"), and permanent ("always"). Whereas a person with more constructive beliefs – who may well be exactly as intelligent, talented and skilled as the destructive person – might say, after a similar mistake, "That's not like me? I wonder what happened. I'll do better next time."

So, let's say that here that our destructive person has underestimated their ability, while our constructive person has arguably overestimated their ability. In both cases, they both believe a lie. However, the first will probably be paralysed by her unkind belief and eventually will stop trying to achieve anything. The latter won't be discouraged, will be more likely to try again, and be more likely to try harder. So, here we have two people, with similar abilities, who end up with two very different destinies.

If we're going to believe a lie, doesn't it make sense to at least believe one that supports you, rather than undermines you? Start paying attention to your inner duck's negative talk. Sift through this quacking, and choose what you take; discard the destructive criticism and embrace the positive. Tell the critical voice to "Shut The Duck Up!" Or ask it for the irrefutable evidence to support its validity. Laugh at it. Imagine it talking in a stupid high-pitched tone. If you make it sound silly, it's nearly impossible to take what it says seriously.

If you believed you couldn't fail, then what would you dare to dream?

hope lies in dreams,
in imagination,
and in the courage of those
who dare to make dreams
into reality.

jonas Salk

Key No.15: Take a Small Step First

Did you know you're more likely to take a big step if you've taken a small step first?

There was a study of 'Foot in the Door' techniques, in California in 1966, by the psychologists Jonathan Freedman and Scott Fraser. In one of their experiments, they went from door to door asking homeowners if they'd be willing to place a huge and ugly sign on their front lawn. The sign was white, with red letters reading "DRIVE CAREFULLY." Only 17% of the homeowners asked agreed to display the sign.

In a second survey, Freedman and Fraser knocked on other doors in the same community. This time, they asked the householder to agree to a much smaller request – to sign a petition, or to display a small card in their window about keeping California beautiful. Two weeks later, the same households were asked by a second person to display the ugly "DRIVE CAREFULLY" sign. This time, 76% of the homeowners agreed to have the sign on their front lawn.

So, what can we learn from this? If you take a small action that you feel is within your scope of capability, and consistent with the self-image you want to portray, then you're far more likely to make larger leaps in the future.

Basically, when the homeowners agreed to the small request and signed the petition, they supported their self-image as a caring citizen. It was easy for the homeowners to feel good because the request was easy to fulfil and posed no personal risks. However, having agreed to the small request, most of the homeowners felt duty-bound to agree to the bigger request; turning it down would contradict their desired self-image of a good citizen.

So, start small and then get ready to take those bigger steps!

Key No.16: Be True To Yourself

**"This above all: to thine own self be true,
And it must follow, as the night the day,
Thou canst not then be false to any man."
(Hamlet; William Shakespeare)**

That's the wise advice that Polonius gives to his son as he embarks on his travels. Many of us go on significant personal journeys into unfamiliar territory, and Polonius's advice is just as relevant to us as it was to his son. But how often is it practised, and just how well do you really know yourself?

To help you understand what's really important to yourself, there's a useful tool created by Irving Janis and Leon Mann called a 'Decisional Balance Sheet,' which will enable you to do this.

A Decisional Balance Sheet is divided into four quadrants:

1) What are the advantages of change?
2) What are the disadvantages of change?
3) What are the disadvantages of not changing?
4) What are the advantages of not changing?

Decisional Balance Sheet

	Disadvantages	Advantages
No Change		
Change		

At first glance, these questions may seem counter-intuitive. How could there possibly be any benefits in not changing, or in living below your potential? Surely there can't be any disadvantages in achieving your goals? But let's say, for example, you value your work, and you cherish the time you spend with your family.

To enable you to work at your best, you decide to get fit, so you start a training programme and vow to exercise three nights a week. This might satisfy your desire to perform at your best at work, but as it costs you three treasured nights a week with your family, then there's a clear clash between your desires.

Take another example; perhaps you're dissatisfied with your physical appearance and discouraged by a lack of energy. Imagine you also have a circle of good friends whose company you enjoy, and whose support you value. You go drinking with these friends in the pub most nights; their friendship is important to you, as is the feeling of belonging and being accepted by them.

You resolve to work on your physical appearance and energy levels by joining a gym. However, your friends' habit of regularly spending evenings in the pub now directly clashes with your aims of getting fit. To achieve your goals, you start skipping the odd evening at the pub to go to the gym, and when you do go to the pub, you're careful to drink less.

Now, suppose that these friends see your new-found commitment to fitness and health as an act of betrayal towards them. They feel that you're rejecting them, and start acting accordingly towards you. So, the better you do on your programme, the more disconnected you begin to feel from your friends. As a result, the closer you get towards your fitness goals, the unhappier you get as you sense you've lost the support of your friends.

The earlier you can anticipate possible consequences, like the examples above, the easier you'll find it to handle them. You might decide to change your strategy altogether; at the very least, you'll be mentally prepared for the challenges that lie ahead. If you can't find an alternative strategy, then you'll need to prioritise what's important to you and then decide whether you really do want to achieve your goal, or whether you'd actually prefer to stick with the status quo.

One way to accomplish this, is to identify the values that matter most to you and why.

Read the list of values below, and choose the five that are most important to you. If there's a particular value that isn't mentioned, just add it to the list. Then, order your five values by importance.

- Relationships
- Love
- Family
- Acceptance
- Creativity
- Confidence
- Financial independence
- Self-expression
- Courage
- Fun
- Excitement
- Passion
- Making a difference
- Serenity
- Security
- Power
- Humour
- Being liked
- Spirituality
- Personal Growth
- Excellence
- Discipline
- Integrity

- Health
- Recognition
- Respect
- Attractiveness
- Resourcefulness
- Education
- Adventure
- Honesty
- Freedom

Next time there's a conflict between your goals, you'll be better equipped to decide which of your values take priority and to act accordingly.

Be sure to consider:

- Which one of these values, if you lived in complete alignment with it, would give your life the greatest meaning and enjoyment?
- How achieving your goals would help you live more consistently with your core values.
- How achieving your goals might detract you from your core values.
- How not achieving your goals would help you live more consistently with your core values.
- How not achieving your goals would detract you from your core values.

These questions can help you get to the root cause of what you truly want.

We often sacrifice our lives for the approval of others, but in the end, we can only be truly happy when we do things for our own reasons. But first, you have to clarify what those reasons are, so you can be true to yourself and live life on your own terms.

Well, if you're true
to yourself
you're going to
be true to
everyone else.

john wooden

Key No.17: No Affirmations, Please!

How many times have you been told to use affirmations to create the life you desire? If you've ever experienced the world of self-help, maybe through a seminar, book or even a tape, you've almost certainly been told that affirmations will create the life you desire.

But what happens if your life isn't transformed to the degree promised? Then, the 'experts' will tell you it's all your fault – you must have let a negative thought into your head, thus cancelling out the positive energy created by the affirmations. Unfortunately, rather than realising that affirmations are actually a load of nonsense, we blame ourselves. Yet again, we tell ourselves that we're miserable failures; which unfortunately just increases our likelihood of further failure.

Ibrahim Senay is a psychologist at the University of Illinois at Urbana-Champaign. His works have recently been featured by the writer Wray Herbert in the magazine *Scientific American Mind*.

Senay examined how our self-talk affects our behaviours with an intriguing experiment. A group of volunteers were split in half. The first group were told to contemplate whether or not they would work on solving some anagrams. The second group was asked to think about the fact that they would be shortly working on solving some anagrams. It's a subtle distinction, but significant, the difference between "Will I do this?" and "I will do this."

Now, which group do you think performed better? Traditionally, wouldn't you expect it to be the second group? After all, they were the group that was given the affirmation.

Surprisingly, it was the first set of volunteers who did the task better. Senay repeated the experiment again and again, and found the same results.

A later experiment involved another two groups of people. The first group was asked to contemplate whether or not they would stick to a new exercise programme. The second group were given an affirmation declaring that they would stick to their new programme.

Again, the results were the same. The group asking, "Will I?" had much more commitment than the group stating, "I will."

So, why would a question be far more effective than a declaration? Senay interviewed his participants to try to find out.

The group that had the question, "Will I?" tended to answer along the lines of, "Because I want to take more responsibility for my own health," whereas the other group ("I Will") answered, "Because I would feel guilty or ashamed of myself if I did not."

Guilt and shame are terrible motivators. They won't encourage you to achieve your goals, and will only leave you feeling, obviously, guilty and ashamed. It's far better to find a genuine desire to achieve the goal.

Here's why we reckon affirmations don't always work:

1. Declarations are final. If we announce "I will," it cuts ourselves off from other possibilities. This can trigger off an irrational fear of loss of freedom; we wind up rebelling against our affirmation to confirm to ourselves that we still have a choice!

2. We're subjective about our past. We might be saying "I will" today, but our mind holds the memories of our failures of the past. We fear being judged or criticised over the gap between what we say and what we do, and that can be enough to stop us from following through on the affirmation.

3. Performance anxiety. Saying "I will" focuses us on the outcome. For example, an affirmation like, "I will lose four stone in weight," is actually quite daunting, and can deter someone from committing fully to their new exercise programme. Whereas "Will I lose four stones?" allows more room for us to concentrate on the process, makes us feel more in control and allow us to approach change at our own pace.

Ask yourself "Will I?" instead of telling yourself "I will."

Key No.18: Love Conquers All

It's funny what we'll tolerate, or even do willingly, for love.

Pete lives in London; whenever he squeezes himself onto a rush-hour Tube, he asks himself why on earth does he put up with it. After all, it's pretty grim having to stand for the whole of your journey, plus being squashed into the window of the door AND often in the company of people who've apparently never heard of deodorant.

So, why does he do it? Because he genuinely loves London. It's where he was born, where his family lives, and he just loves living there.

We have another friend who adores nuts, but never eats them. You might assume that it's because he's allergic to them, but no.

It's actually his wife who's allergic to them; if he ate nuts, he wouldn't be able to kiss her. So, he cheerfully lives a nut-free life, and all for love.

If you do something that you love (or for someone whom you love), it's always easier than for someone who lacks that love.

We tend to be at our most creative, and productive, when we work at something we love.

Do you love what you do? So how do you start your day? Do you wake up and think, "Brilliant?! Another wonderful day ahead; I can't wait to get going?" Or do you wake up in a state of panic, "Oh no, here we go again," battling the morning commute with a feeling of grim resignation?

If the second scenario feels depressingly familiar, then take heart. It doesn't have to be that way, really! Everything you experience literally shapes your brain: everything you learn changes the structure of your brain via synaptic connections.

Try the following suggestions for one week and see what a difference they make to your life.

Every morning, when you wake, ask yourself:

- What am I most grateful for today?
- What opportunities will I capitalise on?
- What do I look forward to learning today?
- How will I make a difference to someone before the day is through?
- What will I receive as a result?
- What do I love the most about my work?
- In what way will I do what I love the most?

Then, spend 15 minutes (at least) doing something that helps your professional development. You could read something related to what you most love about your work, or researching areas that you want to improve. Not everyone works. If you don't, then do this exercise for your hobbies or interests.

At the end of the day, take five minutes to assess:

- What have I learnt today?
- How did I make a difference?
- In what way(s) did I get to do what I love?

When you take control of your focus, you live each day by design, not default.

Do try doing this every day. What you do daily determines who you become permanently!

Key No.19: Blame Is Lame

Have you ever been on a diet that didn't work? We've known people to blame their diet failures on their spouse, on the people who run fast-food chains, even on the evil woman at the office who's always bringing in those bloody cakes.

Is anyone prepared to take responsibility for anything these days? It seems like everyone blames somebody else.

Parents blame the schools for their own children's behaviour. Celebrities blame the media for their own descent into 'booze and drug's hell'. Many people blame the government for pretty much everything. Have you ever blamed your parents for the way you behave?

The philosopher Immanual Kant explained that both blame and praise are perfectly appropriate when they're truly deserved. Often in our lives, however, it's easy to scattergun blame unfairly instead of taking responsibility where we need to. Is blame actually useful, even if it's appropriate and deserved?

Blame isn't a constructive way of giving feedback. Blame breeds guilt. Blame doesn't help people to correct their behaviour. It can even be counter-productive, as it can reinforce a person's belief that they're not capable of change. If you place blame on someone or something else, you're missing an opportunity to change your method to something more effective.

So, it's time to stop blaming other people. That doesn't mean you should blame yourself for everything though. Far from it! You need to stop blaming yourself too, and you need to move on from everything you've ever blamed yourself for in the past. Take a deep breath, and let the guilt go. In future, take responsibility for your actions; you'll be taking control of your life.

if it's never our fault, we can't take responsibility for it. if we can't take responsibility for it, we'll always be its victim.

richard bach

Key No.20: Don't Duck Out Today (Or Any Other Day)

**"What if I didn't have to die?
I would turn every minute into an age;
nothing would be wasted,
every minute would be accounted for..."**

- Fyodor Dostoyevsky, *The Idiot*

In *The Idiot*, Prince Myshkin recalls these words said by a man moments before his execution, although later in the book, we find out that the man was never actually executed. In this case, art imitates life; though the characters in the book are fictitious, Dostoyevsky did experience the trauma of a mock execution many years earlier.

In December 1825, Nicholas I became the Emperor of Russia under somewhat controversial conditions. As the youngest of his brothers, he was never meant to be czar but when his older brother Alexander I, the rightful Emperor of Russia, died suddenly of typhus, Nicholas took the throne.

Almost immediately, the military attempted to overthrow the new czar. Although Nicholas successfully suppressed the Decembrist revolt, he remained sensitive to the possibility of further attempts at revolution, and punished underground organisations harshly.

On April 23rd, 1849, Fyodor Dostoyevsky was arrested for being part of the 'Petrashevsky Circle,' a group of liberal intellectualists.

For months, the members of the circle were held in solitary confinement with no word on what was to become of them. Day after day, month after month, they sat in their cells cut off from the outside world.

On November 16th, the doors of their cells were opened, and Dostoyevsky and his companions were loaded into a carriage. It was a bitterly cold day, but the men were only clad in the spring clothes that they'd been wearing since they were arrested.

They speculated about their possible punishment. They'd already been imprisoned for months; the charges against them were only for the possession and reading of revolutionary materials, and they hadn't actually plotted any acts against the czar, so they assumed that their sentence wouldn't be that harsh.

However, when the men disembarked the carriage, they were horrified to find a priest waiting to give them their last rites. They were to be executed by a firing squad. Hoods were placed over their heads, and they listened to the sound of the rifles being loaded and then the order to take aim.

Dostoyevsky's thoughts were not full of fear as he prepared to die; instead he concentrated on how much he loved and valued his life.

But then, rather than the rifles' fire, they heard the beating of a drum. It announced the arrival of the czar's personal messenger. The men weren't going to be executed. Instead, they were sentenced to four years of hard labour. The whole execution had been staged as the czar never meant to kill the men, but instead to make a point, and what a point! Two members of the Petrashevsky Circle went insane over the mental trauma of the experience; emotionally, and mentally, they died there that day.

As for Fyodor Dostoyevsky, that was the day he was re-born. In a letter he wrote to his brother Mikhail, he said, "When I look back on my past and think how much time I wasted on nothing, how much time has been lost in futilities, errors, laziness, incapacity to live; how little I appreciated it, how many times I sinned against my heart and soul - then my heart bleeds. Life is a gift; life is happiness; every minute can be an eternity of happiness." Dostoyevsky spent his four years in prison. On release, he was forced to serve in the Siberian Regiment for five years. After this, he did, in fact, live his life with a sense of renewed appreciation. Despite suffering many hardships, he became one of most well-known Russian Existentialist writers of his era.

The vast majority of us will never face death for our beliefs. But how many of us will effectively sacrifice our lives by not living them to our fullest potential? The truth is that we duck out of full, productive, exciting days all the time. So now imagine looking back on a career of disappointment and asking ourselves the painfully futile question, "Why?" simply, because we never asked ourselves, "Why not?"

Begin every day with appreciation of what you have,
and live each day creatively.
Refuse to squander your precious time,
not even one minute of it,
and fully commit yourself to the
purpose that you choose.

You know, you only get to live life once, so there are two things that that yields. One is that there's no point in crying over spilt milk, but secondly you hate wasting time, energy, and whatever talent you've got.

david Miliband

Key No.21: Understand Your Impulses

The philosopher Aristotle believed that we should explore our emotional impulses, and then employ them intelligently. While it sounds great in theory, it's far easier said than done.

You might make a decision rationally, but making it into reality is another matter. Have you ever decided to be 'good' and have just a tiny taste of dessert, only to wind up eating the whole thing? Or vowed not to buy anything unnecessary in the sales, but still came home with a credit card smoking from overuse? Or had a friend that's vowed, countless times, to dump her boyfriend, but is still with him months, even years later?

The neuroscientist Joseph Ledoux explains in his book, *The Emotional Brain*, that our emotions have a significant influence over our reasoning. In many cases, our emotions - essentially, the limbic system- overrule the prefrontal lobes that perform our rational thinking.

It might seem strange that emotions should overcome reason, but there's an excellent evolutionary reason for it. In life-threatening situations, we need to react quickly. Our unconscious mind reacts in a flash, whereas it takes a relatively lengthy time to actively think something through and decide what action to take.

Ever burnt yourself on a hot pan or oven? Chances are you whipped your hand away immediately from the source of the heat. It wasn't the rational part of the brain moving your hand; your rational brain would follow a process that goes more like this: "Hey! My hand's hot. Really too hot! Dangerously hot! Must let go of this pan. Ah, that's better," by which time your hand would be seriously injured. Instead, your unconscious mind reacts immediately, and your hand is away from the danger before your conscious brain has even properly realised what's happened.

Your unconscious brain protects you in threatening situations, but what about in everyday life? Well, our emotional impulses can be rather inconvenient. Your sensible brain urges us to make better food choices and save for the future, while your unconscious brain yearns to party:

"Go on, let's live on cheese footballs and arctic roll! Let's go buy another handbag; we're only a little overdrawn! You deserve it!"

What's a modern, health-conscious person to do? Well, one helpful strategy is Metacognition. This means to think about, and to question, your thoughts.

When the limbic system (i.e. the combined brain structures, like the amygdala, hypothalamus and the cingulate gyrus that supports emotions and behaviour) is running the show, the desire for pleasure and the need to avoid pain dominates nearly everything. From that, we can deduce that the desire to eat a whole tub of Häagen-Dazs, or skip a workout, or keep spending when we're already in debt, is linked to the gap between how we feel and how we desire to feel.

Here's a really useful tool: simply stop and ask yourself what your motives are for doing or not doing something. For example, next time you instinctively reach for a doughnut, ask yourself the following questions:

- Why am I eating this?
- How do I feel right now?
- How do I want to feel after I eat this?
- How else can I feel that way without having to eat this?

The answers may well help you come up with an alternative course of action. If you want to feel comforted, then maybe you could call a close friend instead. Or give yourself a non-food treat, like a bubble bath with your favourite magazine.

Sometimes, you don't need to do anything at all. It's enough to just acknowledge how you're feeling, without needing to act on it in any way.

At the very least, asking these questions will give you some breathing space, and stop you merely eating the doughnut without thinking. If, after working through the questions, you're still adamant that you have to eat, then go for it; only be sure to do it with a clear conscience, to enjoy every mouthful, and to stop eating as soon as you've had enough. You may well find that just a single taste is enough.

Anything worth doing is worth doing well. Even if you stumble some of the time – and chances are, you will – with effort and consistent work, you'll get better and better at it. Eventually, you'll find that your impulses work for you, rather than against you.

~

Key No.22: A Tiny Advantage Can Make a Ten-Fold Difference

When water's heated to 100 degrees, it starts to boil,
which creates steam.
With steam, you can move a locomotive.

When water's heated to 99 degrees,
it's almost as hot. But it doesn't boil,
so no steam,
and no related power.

A difference of one degree makes all the difference in the world.

If a horse wins a race – even by just a nose - that horse will typically earn several times more prize money than the second-place horse. But the winning horse isn't several times faster than the horse that comes second. It's not even twice as fast. It's only a fraction better, yet the reward it earns is so much greater.

Often, the difference between mediocrity and competency is a small one; a slight edge applied effectively and continually. A slight edge in performance creates remarkable results.

The book *The Inspiring Leader: Unlocking the Secret of How Extraordinary Leaders Motivate*, by John Zenger, Joseph Folkman and Scott Edinger, is great for those keen to learn what separates extraordinary leaders from ordinary leaders. In the book, they used 360-degree feedback tools to describe 20,000 managers, and identified one particular trait within the managers who produced the best results with their teams. The "silver bullet," so to speak, "inspires and motivates to high performance."

Their findings are surprising. Obviously, throughout history, there have been many charismatic and inspiring leaders. For example, John F. Kennedy, Dr. Martin Luther King Jr. and Winston Churchill. There have also been others who were not inspiring in the traditional sense of being a 'motivator'. Instead, they motivated others through a compelling vision: Mother Theresa and Mahatma Ghandi, amongst others, are examples.

Before reading Zenger's book, both of us would have assumed that an extraordinary leader had to be a brilliant strategist; someone who could gather and mobilise resources. We knew that the ability to motivate would have been part of the success story, but we hadn't realised that it was actually much more than this. Rather than being just a component, the ability to motivate is the factor that separated the ordinary from the extraordinary, but is it really possible for another person to motivate us for a long period of time? Don't we burn out or lose the faith?

In their book *Primal Leadership*, Daniel Goleman, Richard Boyatzis and Annie McKee say: "Great leaders move us. They ignite our passion and inspire the best in us. When we try to explain why they are so effective, we speak of strategy, vision or powerful ideas. But the reality is much more primal; great leadership works through the emotions. [...] Even if they get everything else just right, if leaders fail in this primal task of driving emotions in the right direction, nothing will work as well as it could or should."

Primal Leadership looked at leadership not just from an organisational level, but from a neurological one as well. Effective leadership isn't a matter of a leader's ability to perform, so much as his ability to get others to perform; this has a much greater yield in production.

They also point out an assertion of the late management expert Peter Drucker. If most businesses increased the productivity of each employee by just 10%, they would double their profits. Clearly, the ability to inspire a 10% increase in the productivity is a hugely valuable one.

Sir Alex Ferguson, the legendary Manchester United football manager, utilised this skill during his 27 years leading one of most successful teams in the British Premiership (and the most widely supported soccer clubs in the world as well). As Pete worked with a number of top British professional football teams including Arsenal and Fulham, he had met Sir Alex on the occasions when the teams were playing against each other. He often asked him, "What's the secret of your success?" but Sir Alex never told him. Only after he had retired and they bumped into each other again did he finally tell Pete. Sir Alex's secret was to get everyone to play for him.

Like all true leaders, he set standards for his players to live up to and let them know that he believed in them. He empowered them and in doing so, Sir Alex's players would perform at their best, knowing a high performance was expected of them.

Seek out people who make you feel motivated; being around them will keep you motivated, and you will perform to a higher standard. You'll also absorb the message that it's okay to be excited, to be motivated, to express yourself, to be free to be your personal best! And when you allow yourself to be your best, you'll in turn motivate others to do the same.

if your actions inspire others to dream more, learn more, do more and become more, you are a leader.

john quincy adams

Key No.23: Act Happy, Be Happy

In their book *Unmasking the Face*, the researchers Paul Ekman and Wallace Friesen demonstrated that our body language and facial expressions can affect how we feel. That's because they correspond with centres of the brain that profoundly influence our mood. When you genuinely smile, it gives you a rush of happiness.

Another book that intrigued me was *Emotional Contagion*. The authors, Hatfield, Cocioppo and Rapson, explained that not only do our body language and facial expressions control our emotional state, they're contagious as well. This makes sense if you think about it. Have you ever been in a really good mood, but then spent time with a friend who was upset about something? It's pretty impossible to retain your high spirits in that situation, and you probably found yourself feeling pretty sad too after a while.

Human beings have an innate tendency to mirror the body language and facial expressions of others, especially if it is someone who we admire or want to please. This leads us to feel the same emotions as them. To be clear; it's not that the speaker is so energetic or charismatic that they ignite the emotion in us, it's that in mirroring them, we're sending our brain messages that are similar to the ones they're sending, and so we start feeling similarly to the way they do.

If you want to change your mood, change your physiology.

attitudes are contagious. Make sure yours is worth catching.

Key No.24: Adapt To Survive

One evening in April 1970, NASA received a radio communication from Apollo 13's commander: "OK, Houston, we've had a problem here" (yes, it's endlessly misquoted as ,"Houston, we have a problem"!).

It was quite the understatement; it was actually a rather ominous situation. Over 250,000 miles from Earth, hurtling through space, Command Module Pilot Jack Swigert reported that an explosion and numerous malfunctions had caused the Apollo to lose power and one of her oxygen tanks. The crew was adrift in space, at sub-zero temperatures, with no clear way home. Although they had a number of options, all of them were incredibly risky.

Eventually, the astronauts decided to continue their flight path heading straight for the moon. The astronauts, and the scientists at NASA, reasoned that they could use the gravitational pull of the moon as a slingshot to thrust them back to Earth.

It was a brilliant plan, but a dangerous one. If they miscalculated any of the variables pertaining to speed, angle or distance during their approach, they would either crash or overshoot the moon, leaving them permanently stranded in space.

After days of worry and stress, a team of exhausted engineers were elated as the Apollo capsule and parachutes appeared over the southern Pacific Ocean. Their calculations had been perfect, and the crew were saved.

It wasn't anyone's fault that the Apollo had nearly been lost; everyone prepared diligently.

Regardless of how well-laid our plans may be, sometimes there are more variables than we can predict. In these instances, the plans you have are worthless, unless they can be adapted. If the Apollo crew hadn't adapted their plans, they would have died.

the worst part of success is,
to me, adapting to it.
it's scary.

kendrick lamar

Key No.25: It's all about the Journey, Not the Destination.

Ever felt like this: "I want to have patience, and I WANT IT NOW!" It's something that I see a lot in my work. I'll have a client who's making gradual and steady progress towards their goals, but because they don't appreciate the hard work they've done and want to get to their goal immediately, they give up. They'll probably try again sometime, and again, get some of the way but give up because they're not seeing instant results. They're doomed to 'almost succeed' over and over again. Eventually, they stop trying.

The secret of success is to work constantly. It doesn't have to be hard work; it just has to be consistent. It's what we do daily that determines the results we produce indefinitely.

There once was a very wealthy man who had twin boys. On their eighteenth birthday, he called them into his study. "Since you both were children, I have tried my best to teach you the many lessons I learnt over the years, hoping they would serve you as they did me," he said. "Yet, some lessons cannot be passed on; they must be learnt from experience."

He told them how he wanted to give them a proper start in life, and hoped they would always make wise decisions. On top of his desk, he had two boxes, containing their birthday presents. "In one box is one million pounds in cash, in the other is a shiny penny." He explained. "If you choose the million pounds, you can have it right now and do with it as you please," he continued, "but if you choose the penny, I will have my accountant double the amount every day, for thirty days. After that, the money is yours to keep."

The first born of the twins immediately said, "I'll have the million in cash, of course!" With that, his father hugged him, handed him the box, and told him to use it well.

The businessman turned to his other son and asked, "Do you want a million in cash as well?" The son was tempted, as that was more money than he had ever seen at once. However, he knew his father was a clever man who relished in passing on wisdom to his children. There had to be a lesson in all of this. "Father, I will take the penny."

His father smiled and made an appointment for the son to meet him in the study exactly one month from that day.

If you had to make the same decision, which box would you choose? The day after, true to his father's word, the younger twin had two pence. Then, four pence, eight pence, sixteen pence. By day seven, he was feeling rather discouraged; his brother had a million pounds, and he had only 64p! After fourteen days, he had just £81.92. However, the sum continued to double every day. By day 26, he had £335,544.32!

On the last day of the month, the younger twin was astonished when the accountant informed him that he'd amassed a fortune of £5,368,709.12!

This isn't just a lesson in maths, but in patience as well. 'Compounding effort' in this way is a lesson in life that many of us understand, yet few of us practice.

Have you ever started a new health regime, worked incredibly hard for a few days (maybe even a few weeks!), then lost your motivation and gave up? You're not alone. Gyms lose an astonishingly high level of their members. People quit when they don't see progress instantly.

Everything worth achieving requires work, consistency and patience. It doesn't matter where you are on day three of your programme. What matters is where you are on day 300 and, further on, day 3,000.

The realisation of our goals is often sabotaged by the need for instant gratification. The thing is that instant gratification is important - even essential – in the achievement of many goals.

But that gratification must be found in the process, and not just the outcome.

Say you start a new exercise programme, because you want to lose a few pounds in weight. On day three, you weigh yourself. You are desperate to see some weight loss, even though you know that's unrealistic. You decide that you'll settle for the instant gratification having lost a few pounds.

Again, you know full well that's unrealistic, but you convince yourself that's a possibility as you step onto the scales. You look at the reading... and your weight, of course, hasn't changed a jot. You're likely to feel despondent, or even drawn to comfort eat, feeling that your efforts have come to nothing.

You need to change your mindset. Your gratification shouldn't come from the actual weight loss. It needs to come from the knowledge that you are working hard and making an effort to take care of yourself, and that the weight loss you desire will come along as a result of these changes. Take your satisfaction from the journey, and not just the destination!

If you're faced with a task that seems enormous, break it down into chunks. Create small and achievable daily goals. They'll soon stack up into big achievements. What we do daily determines who we become permanently.

Ask yourself these questions every day, before you go to sleep, to stay on track:

Was I better today than I was yesterday?

Did I do what I said I was going to do?

Did I do it well?

And, every month, ask yourself:

What one daily goal can I add to achieve more and become more?

It's often not the huge declarations that produce the greatest change; it's the little things done daily— but compounded over time—that produce the most remarkable change.

Little men with little minds and little imaginations go through life in little ruts, smugly resisting all changes which would jar their little worlds.

Zig Ziglar

Key No.26: Sleep Your Way to the Top

Bobby used to be a fitness manager. Every day, his alarm clock would blast him out of bed at 4am, then he'd play a little game to make the early start more bearable. Could he beat his personal record for getting dressed? Kettle on. Shower. Shave. Clothes. On a good morning, he could do it in 25 minutes.

He'd grab a flask of coffee and dash to the car. He had to be on time as the gym opened every morning at 5am and the first client of the day would be expecting him. He'd see five clients in a row, have a bite to eat, and start his management duties. He'd regularly work until 10.30pm.

Have you ever worked similar, crazily long hours? Or, maybe, as a new parent, staying awake for what feels like months on end, getting through the days on little or no sleep? Ever wondered, looking back, how you coped? How did you get through it? Youth? Passion? Buckets of coffee?

When Bobby thinks about those days, he remembers a habit that he used to have back then. He'd take a late lunch every afternoon and then go back home for a 45-minute nap, which was enough to refresh him and keep him going into the night.

This completely went against all the professional advice he'd received! Work alone, without interruption, if you want to be truly successful. Get up as early as possible, work late into the night, study, learn your way to success. The message was clear: sleep is for losers! And that message was wrong.

A little rest can give you back your focus, stamina and improve your performance. Confucius said, "A workman must sharpen his tools if he is to do his work well." But this doesn't just apply at the start of the day; it applies throughout the day as well. After all, an axe will go blunt during the course of a day's work. The workman needs to stop and sharpen it. It's the same with our bodies and our minds. We can't use them constantly, we have to stop to refresh ourselves.

The neuroscientist Matthew Walker conducted an experiment into memory. Volunteers were taught to move their fingers in patterns; these patterns mimicked piano scales. Half the subjects were then instructed to have a nap for around an hour, while the other half stayed awake and continued with the rest of their day. Later, the volunteers were all re-testing on the finger patterns. The people that had napped performed 16% better than those who'd stayed awake. That's a pretty remarkable result.

Have you ever heard the saying, "An hour's sleep before midnight is worth two after"? Turns out there's plenty of truth in that. Walker explains that "a daytime power nap produces nearly as much off-line memory enhancement as a whole night of sleep." This is because "the brain selectively increases spindle activity in local brain circuits, thereby discretely targeting those regions in the brain that have recently formed new memories. Sleep spindles appear to make a selective and critical contribution to improving our motor memories at night and across power naps during the day."

The long-distance yachtswoman, Dame Ellen MacArthur, used 'power naps' throughout her solo circumnavigation of the globe. As she was sailing single-handedly, Dame Ellen wasn't able to sleep for any long length of time. She came to Pete for help in figuring out how she could both sail and sleep while out on the ocean. They decided that while she would sleep for 15 minute bursts, just prior to nodding off, she would tell herself that these 15 minutes would be the equivalent of eight hours of deep, restful shut-eye. This really worked. By using the power of the mind in tandem with the energising capabilities of short napping, Dame Ellen was able to maintain the energy, focus and alertness that she needed to complete her historic journey.

Now we know that power napping sounds great in theory, but how many of us actually have the luxury of all that spare time? The good news is that these power naps can actually be extremely short. All you need is a comfortable place where you can close your eyes and rest for about 10 to 20 minutes. Maybe during your lunch break? Make the time, because it's a 15-minute investment that will yield hours of high-performance work.

Albert Einstein used frequent naps to support his mental performance. So, if it worked for Einstein, isn't it worth having a try? Sweet dreams!

My father said there were two kinds of people in the world: givers and takers. the takers may eat better, but the givers sleep better.

Marlo thomas

Key No.27: Don't Feed the Ducks

Long ago, there lived an old Cherokee. Knowing that he didn't have long to live, he devoted his time to teaching his young grandson about life.

While walking together one day, the grandfather spoke to his grandson. "A fight is going on inside of me. It is a terrible fight, and it is between two warring wolf spirits. One is evil; he is anger, envy, sorrow, regret, greed, arrogance, self-pity, resentment, lies, false pride, and ego. The other is good; he is joy, peace, love, hope, serenity, humility, kindness, benevolence, empathy, generosity, truth, compassion, and faith. The same fight is going on inside of you."

The boy thought about this for a moment. "Grandpa, which one will win?" The old Cherokee simply responded, "Whichever one you feed."

We all have internal struggles to contend with. Ever felt like you really did have an angel and a devil on your shoulders? One voice telling you to do the right thing, the other telling you to do exactly what you want? We've all experienced the cause and effect relationship our choices have to their consequences.

Some of us are especially torn between what we know we should do, and what we actually do. How can it be that if someone knows that they're unhappy, if they desperately want to change, and need to change, that they'll then do the very things that stand in the way of change? The short answer is: because we're only human.

As for the long answer: from our childhood onwards, we develop beliefs. Many of these are subconscious, but all of them are powerful, and these beliefs give meaning to the world around us. They create the mental maps that we use to navigate the world, and they affect our perception of what's safe, what's dangerous, what's desirable, and what's important.

Every experience that you've ever had caused neurons in your brain to communicate both electrically and chemically, and your beliefs affected your interpretation of those experiences. Two people going through the same experience will learn different lessons from it. In turn, the lessons we learn affect the formation of new connections in our brains.

The psychologist Donald Hebb coined the term "neurons that fire together wire together." This means that neural networks will become stronger and bigger the more frequently that they're stimulated. Also, the more emotional relevance that's attached to the triggering event, the more the network strengthens and grows. As the neural networks in our brains get bigger and stronger, the more profoundly they affect who we are.

If you feel you sometimes struggle against yourself - if you'd love to make positive changes to your life, but seem to sabotage your every attempt at a new life - don't forget that you've been conditioned to be the way you are for a very long time.

As a result, we distort the world around us. 'Automatic Negative Thoughts' are a concept pioneered by the psychologist Aaron T. Beck back in the late 1960s. Do any of the examples below sound familiar to you?

Overgeneralisation: Sarah would love to get fitter. She goes to her local gym, where a trainer suggests that she try a particular group class. Sarah replies, "That won't work for me. I've tried them before." She goes on to think to herself, "I'm too out of shape, so the instructor won't want me in her class. I'd probably struggle to keep up with the class, and the instructor wouldn't help me; those sorts of people are all superficial and self-absorbed."

Mental Filter: John started an exercise programme last month. He's been on time for every session so far. But today, traffic was unusually bad and he was ten minutes late. He says to himself, "I'm just not disciplined. This is why I always fail."

Disqualification: Mary has been training for three months. Yesterday at the office, a co-worker mentioned how well she looked. She explains it away by saying, "Oh, it's the outfit I am wearing. I bought it to hide how fat I am."

Magnification: Peter performs especially well in a presentation he gave to the marketing department at the office. However, there was one question he didn't know the answer to straight away. When his boss later compliments him on his great work, he says, "I didn't do so well, I need to work harder; I really blew it."

Emotional Reasoning: Jane's just joined a gym and has had a health assessment. She's reviewing all the dietary changes she needs to make, and working out how much time she'll have to spend at the gym each week. Jane feels that the demands on her are so overwhelming, it's simply hopeless, and she's bound to fail. Why even try?

Labelling: Sally's just cheated on her diet. Disgusted with herself, she tells herself that she is nothing but a fat, lazy pig.

Personalisation: Dave's late for a date with Rachel because he's stuck on the tube. While waiting, Rachel tells herself that Dave's not made the effort to turn up on time, because she's not that much of a catch.

Clearly, these thoughts are destructive, and not in the least bit helpful for anyone trying to achieve anything!

If you suffer from this sort of inner duck talk, then here's a technique that could help. Consider pretending for just a week that you're someone else who's got the skill you want to have. Maybe you've got a friend whose confidence you've always envied. It doesn't even have to be someone whom you know personally; you could model a celebrity.

Then work through these steps:

1. Be conscious of your thinking. Notice when your brain comes up with an 'Automatic Negative Thought.'

2. Take responsibility for the thought. Ask yourself, "Is this the type of thought that my role model would have?"

3. Replace the thought with something more positive. Now ask yourself, "What's my role model likely to be thinking? What other thought could I choose to have?"

4. Find an appropriate, supportive thought, then act in a way that's in keeping with this thought.

5. Tell someone supportive about the persona that you're adopting for the week. This is so they can encourage you, and that you're held responsible by others who care about you as well.

After a week of modelling, you should notice that your 'Automatic Negative Thoughts' decrease. Feel free to keep repeating the experiment for as long as you want. Just remember; even if negative thoughts pop into your head, you don't have to feed them. It's up to you which voice you want to listen to. If you don't want to listen to that duck quacking away, then you know what to do: starve it of your attention, and eventually it'll shut the duck up!

Key No.28: Don't Mistake Your Strength for a Weakness

Here's a true tale that we want to share with you. They were much like any other family, until their nine-year-old son tragically lost his left arm in a car accident. Unsurprisingly, this was a huge blow to the child, who had once been energetic and cheerful. A year later, he was still depressed, lacked confidence, and was seemingly disinterested in everything.

His worried parents kept trying to lift his spirits, and searched for something that interested him, but had no success. They wondered if their son would ever be the same again.

One day, the boy came home from school and announced that he wanted to try judo. His parents were thrilled that something had sparked his interest, but also concerned. Would he ever be able to win anything with just one arm? Would he constantly be humiliated? Maybe he'd even get hurt?

Despite their worries (they didn't want to discourage him), they sent him to the local dojo. The judo master there assured them that the boy would be fine, as long as he agreed to do whatever he was told. Lessons began and the boy soon learnt his first move. He was so keen that he practised that move every chance he had.

After three months, the boy was confused and frustrated. He still only knew one technique. The master complimented the boy on his diligence and encouraged him to stay focused, but still didn't teach him any other moves. As each lesson passed, his disappointment grew.

"Sensei," the boy finally said, "shouldn't I be learning more moves?"

The master replied, "This may be the only move you know, but it is the only move you'll ever need to know." The boy believed in his teacher, even if he didn't quite understand the answer, and he kept training. Several months later, the sensei took the boy to his first tournament.

The boy easily won his first two matches, pinning his opponents to the mat with ease. The crowd exploded into applause. They'd never seen such skill, not least from a boy with only one arm. The third match was tougher, but eventually his opponent became impatient and charged. The boy deftly used his one move, pinned his opponent down, and won the match. The boy was through to the finals, he and his parents amazed by his success. The crowd was behind him, cheering him on. For the first time in a long while, the boy felt truly confident.

In the final, however, the boy's opponent was even bigger, stronger and more experienced than the boys he'd faced before. For a while, it looked like the boy was out of his depth, and might even be in danger of getting injured. The referee was about to stop the match when the sensei intervened, "Let him continue."

The match resumed, everyone in the audience rapt. The two boys faced each other again. The opponent made a critical mistake and dropped his guard momentarily. Instantly, the boy used his move to pin him: the match was over. He had won.

The crowd were on their feet, roaring their approval, astounded at what they'd seen. Members of the audience surged forward, raising the boy onto their shoulders, parading him like a hero, while he cried tears of relief and joy. The parents were proud beyond measure.

Afterwards, the boy sought out his master. "Sensei, how did I win the tournament with only one move?" The judo master answered his student: "Two reasons. One, you've almost mastered one of the most difficult throws in all of judo. Secondly, the only known defence for that move is for your opponent to grab your left arm."

Maybe your greatest strength comes from something you see as a weakness.

Examine your self-image.
What do you see as your weaknesses, and why?
Ask yourself how these traits have influenced your life.
Maybe they have bought you experiences that you
wouldn't have otherwise had.
Maybe, through these weaknesses,
you've learnt coping strategies that have
benefited you in other ways.

∾

Key No.29: Wait For the Fruit to Grow

There's a wonderful quotation:

> ### "The roots of education are bitter,
> ### but the fruits are sweet."

Maybe your school days immediately spring to mind, but this quotes about more than just that.

Every time you face a new situation, every time you learn something new, it can be a painful experience. Ultimately, however, you'll learn something from it that will make your life a sweeter place.

Key No.30: Stop Stressing, Start Moving, Start Living

Have you ever really wanted something, but talked yourself out of it? Maybe there's someone whom you always had a soft spot for, but you never asked them out because you were convinced they'd turn you down.

So many people never reach their potential because they're so terrified of the prospect of failure, rejection or humiliation that it completely paralyses them.

A while ago, we were asked to develop a training course to help new entrepreneurs get going. There are many people out there with all the knowledge and skills to build a very successful company, but their fears are preventing them from doing so. Instead of getting started, many people procrastinate, distract themselves, and even completely shut down. We wanted to help.

We put together a programme that focused on how movement affects emotion. Maybe that sounds strange to you, but it's true, moving about can really change your mood and our findings backed that up. We told our students to exercise every day before starting work. The overwhelming feedback from them was that their new daily routine made them feel more optimistic, energetic, confident and able to take action.

So why does stress cause us to lock up, and why does exercise help us to achieve our goals?

When we're anxious about a particular task, our hypothalamus releases a hormone called Corticotropin Releasing Factor (CRF), followed by Adrenocorticotropic hormone (ACTH). In turn, this exacerbates our anxiety, and floods our bodies with cortisol. Again, this adds to our sense of fear, temporarily impairing function of the frontal lobe, rendering us less effective. When we're less productive and less able to perform, we feel even more anxious about taking a course of action and become even less likely to act.

Conversely, when we get moving, the exercise causes Atrial Natriuretic Peptides (ANP) to be released. ANP mediates the activity in the Hypothalamic-Pituitary Adrenal (HPA) axis in our brain. The HPA axis regulates cortisol release and, therefore, our perceived anxiety levels.

ANP has a calming effect on our bodies. When we can relax, we are better able to concentrate, to evaluate ourselves, and to change our performance. All these factors help us get to our desired results.

We can see actions like exercise as coping mechanisms. They might not directly solve the problems that you're facing, but they'll certainly help you cope better with the situation, which will eventually lead you to solve the problem.

The neuroscientist Joseph LeDoux, of New York University, has researched this area extensively. He asserts that 'active coping' (e.g. exercising) is a far superior alternative to our natural inclination to passively worry.

Active coping reduces our fear levels, which then helps us take the action that we really need to take in life to get from where we are to where we want to be.

If you need a little more persuading, here are more reasons why it's great to exercise, most days:

Mental conditioning: When we exercise, we alter the neuro-chemical environment that inhibits performance. Our mood alters, and we prepare to perform at a higher level.

Mental resilience: It's easy to feel overwhelmed and powerless. Exercising conditions our mind to take action. It encourages a bias for action over passive worry.

Mental substitution: When your mind is focused on something that demands attention, it is then less able to focus on fear, anxiety, worry and other negative emotions that hold us back.

The results you produce reflect the brain that you have. If you want to make changes in your life, you must make changes in your brain. Once you know what you want to do, condition your mind to do it.

If you feel stuck in your life, overcome your physical inertia and get moving! It'll help you overcome your mental inertia. As you exercise your body, you build momentum. In your daily life, as in physics, the more momentum you build, the more unstoppable you become.

∾

Key No.31: Find Your Comfort Blanket

The world can feel like a brutal place sometimes. Whether you've had an upsetting day, heard some bad news, or you're just feeling exhausted, it's important to have something to do that soothes you. Ever seen a toddler with their treasured comfort blanket? These magic bits of fabric can tend to accompany their little owner everywhere, and can fix any crisis. You're never too old to have one!

Bobby's comfort blanket is a trip to the cinema. He finds so many films inspiring, and a great escape from the stresses of life. Seeing a film can even help him get some perspective on his life and any issues he's facing.

There's a brilliant Woody Allen film called *Midnight in Paris*. It's about a Hollywood screenwriter called Gil (played superbly by Owen Wilson) who lives a life of quiet despair. He and his fiancée are a complete mismatch. They both want different things out of life, and she dismisses Gil's dreams of writing a novel.

While they are on holiday in Paris, he falls in love with the city. His imagination carries him back to the Paris of the 1920s, when the city was home to creative legends like Ernest Hemingway, F. Scott Fitzgerald, Salvador Dali and Pablo Picasso. Indeed, he then magically travels back in time to live that exact fantasy. The time he spends with his heroes changes his perspective on his own reality.

For Bobby, the magic moment of that film is when the writer Gertrude Stein, played by the masterful Kathy Bates, reads a draft of Gil's novel. She tells him off for his resigned attitude: "You have a clear and lovely voice. Don't be such a defeatist... the artist's job is not to succumb to despair but to find an antidote for the emptiness of existence."

We love the thought that each of us is actually an artist: the human mind as a canvas, and our knowledge and skills are our palette of colours. Our tools make our lives more beautiful.

Do you have a passion or a hobby? Something you enjoy doing, making or watching? Find something that brings you comfort when the world is cold.

Key No.32: Just Paddle

Ever been so stressed about something that it actually prevented you from dealing with the thing that you're stressed about? It's incredibly common, for example, for people worried about debts to be too scared to even open their mail.

They're worried because they don't want to face what they owe, but, as a result, their credit card and bank statements pile up unpaid. They could be taking positive action by paying off what they can or seeking help. Instead, they do nothing and make their situation worse.

Your problems are always worse in your imagination than they are in reality. Start facing them, paddle towards them. When you start doing something about them, no matter how small, you'll start feeling better.

We cannot solve our problems with the same thinking we used when we created them.

albert einstein

Key No.33: The Work Is Its Own Reward

How do you motivate yourself to do something? Maybe you promise yourself a nice treat when it's done? And if you have kids, do you do sticker charts with them? Your efforts might actually be backfiring; there's actually plenty of research that suggests that the task itself should be its own reward.

Back in 1949, Professor Harry F. Harlow, from the University of Wisconsin, stumbled upon an unusual aspect of behaviour during an experiment. He was studying how rhesus monkeys learn. To do this, he planned to teach the monkeys the whole puzzle by breaking the task down into smaller, simpler chunks. The monkeys would learn each stage over time. When they got each stage right, they'd get a reward.

Well, that was the theory. Instead, something rather unexpected happened.

As soon as they were introduced to the puzzle, the monkeys started to try to solve it for themselves. There was no prompting from the researchers, no prior instruction, and the reward system hadn't even been introduced.

Dr. Harlow realised that the challenge of the problem-solving process was its own reward: the monkeys appeared to be enjoying themselves, and that in itself was all the motivation that they needed.

There's an excellent book, *Irrationality* by the psychologist Stuart Sutherland, which examines our behaviour. Sutherland devotes a chapter to studying rewards, and cites research that shows that awarding people for their performance can actually demotivate them. He talks of a group of children who are asked to do some drawing, and then rewarded for their efforts. Obviously, drawing is a fun and desirable activity in itself, but after the children are rewarded for drawing, they are less likely to want to draw next time. Giving a reward can make the recipient (even small children) subconsciously feel that the activity must be unpleasant in some way, because we're effectively being bribed to do it.

Maybe, as a child, you had to finish your greens before you had your dessert? It's a common parent trick. Did it teach you to love your greens by association with the tasty reward? It's far more likely that instead, this system of bribing taught you to regard greens as an unpleasant 'punishment,' and the dessert as the delicious 'bribe.'

This pattern of thinking tends to stick for life. Do you still regard chocolate as a treat, and broccoli as something that must be tolerated? Really, they're just types of food that fulfil different nutritional needs, but many of us still have those emotionally loaded associations with them. You'll hear people saying they ate a whole tub of ice cream or a whole tub of biscuits because they were sad. We don't think anyone's ever eaten a bunch of carrots just because they were miserable.

That's because sugary, fatty foods, like biscuits and ice cream, have a significant effect on our serotonin and reward pathways. Therefore, what we eat affects how we feel. Given the biochemical effect of food in addition to the psychological effect of our associations to it, no wonder some people find it quite difficult to get comfort without the calories. Changing our associations to food can alleviate a good bit of our struggle with it, while at the same time affording ourselves greater choices in regard to changing the way we feel; even in the absence of it.

When you come across a task that you're dreading, think about the benefit of completing it. For example, decluttering and cleaning a room means that you'll have a pleasant living space at the end of it.

Don't assume you have to reward every task. Next time you're faced with a job that you don't want to do, try just getting on with it and seeing how you feel at the end of it. Hopefully, you'll find the relief of sorting it, or the benefit the task brings, is a reward in itself. Take pride in the job and the achievement itself, otherwise you may distort a run-of-the-mill activity into something that seems actively unpleasant.

Key No.34: Don't Put Off 'Til Tomorrow What You Can Enjoy Today

Have you ever been asked that interview cliché, "Where do you see yourself in five years' time?" It's a ridiculous question, really. The premise is that we should be so disciplined that we make things happen in our life, rather than just letting them happen. In reality, regardless of how disciplined or successful we are, most of us can't predict what our lives will look like even five weeks from now.

The major problem with being a forward thinker is that it takes you out of the present. Some people are so busy thinking about what they're going to be doing, and what they're going to have in the future, that they're utterly unable to appreciate and enjoy the lives that they actually do have in the present. And if they ever do achieve their goal of the big house, the important job, or the large salary, they're still unable to stop and enjoy themselves as there are yet more goals to be reached: the bigger house, the better job, the larger salary.

There's a poignant scene in the film *Sideways*. Miles, one of the lead characters, has been holding onto a bottle of 1961 Cheval Blanc for so long that it was in danger of spoiling. When asked why he hadn't enjoyed it long before, he explains that he's just waiting for a special occasion. His companion Maya counters with "The day you open a '61 Cheval Blanc; that's the special occasion."

Take some time to appreciate the things you actually do have, rather than resenting the things that you don't have yet. The things that make life special are right here, right now. Why wait?

Key No.35: If it's Not Important, Let It Go

**"To be or not to be: that is the question: Whether 'tis nobler in the mind to suffer
The slings and arrows of outrageous fortune,
Or take arms against a sea of troubles,
And by opposing end them?"
- Hamlet; William Shakespeare**

Life is full of trials and struggles. But what's important isn't what those trials are; it's how you react to them that really matters. Some people claim that they're unlucky, or that "everyone" is out to get them. But the "slings and arrows of outrageous fortune" that most of us suffer aren't really the result of conspiracies, or others' schemes. More likely, it's a bit of bad fortune that we've blown out of all proportion. And your mindset really can make all the difference.

In the December 2007 edition of *Discover Magazine*, the author Kathleen McGowan asks the question "Can we cure ageing?" in her article of the same name.

She tells the story of Jim Hammond, who is 93 years old. He's not just in good health, he's an elite athlete. He exercises for hours each day with his trainer; weight training, sprinting, running. He has three gold medals, one silver in amateur competitions, four national racing medals, and a resting heart rate of 50 beats per minute. That'd be impressive for a man half his age!

So, what is the key to slowing the aging process? There's plenty of intriguing theories as to why some of us age faster (and suffer more) than others. Some of the most fascinating research involves Inflammatory Factors.

To briefly explain; there is a protein called 'C-reactive protein' (CPR), which is found in the blood, and its levels rise in response to inflammation in the body. Inflammation isn't the same as infection; it's a protective attempt by an injured body to start the healing process. The presence of raised levels of CPR is an Inflammatory Factor.

McGowan quotes Russell Tracy, Professor of Pathology and Biochemistry at the University of Vermont College of Medicine. He says, "inflammatory factors predict virtually all bad outcomes in humans...It predicts having heart attacks, having heart failure, becoming diabetic; It predicts becoming fragile in old age; predicts cognitive dysfunction, even cancer to a certain extent."

A related theory proposed by Elizabeth Blackburn (*Discover Magazine's* 'Scientist of the Year' in 2007) is that the rate of telomere division affects aging. The telomere is a structure that protects chromosomes from deteriorating, or from fusing with other chromosomes; its division rate appears to be adversely affected by Inflammation.

So, what can reduce inflammation? McGowan suggests that "... healthy food, exercise, and a good attitude" are all helpful. So, yes, our perception of a situation, and our reaction to it are just as important to the longevity and quality of life as our diet and exercise!

We face numerous insults and challenges in our daily lives, whether real or imagined. It's not just our lives that are affected by the decisions we make; the people we care about and rely on are also influenced by the example we set.

It's obvious that if certain behaviour cultivates an internal environment which facilitates "...heart attacks, having heart failure, becoming diabetic, [...] cognitive dysfunction, even cancer, to a certain extent," then it's completely undesirable. So, what can you do instead?

Here are seven questions that you can ask yourself to help discover alternative choices when you face a stressful situation:

1. Is this situation within my control?

However upsetting a situation may be, getting upset doesn't help you deal with it effectively. If you can change your situation, that will probably serve you better than just wasting energy on feeling bad, but not doing anything about it. If the situation is completely outside your control, then remember that this too shall pass, and try to save yourself some stress and aggravation.

2. If I were the other person, what might my intentions be?

It's easy to put your own interpretation on events. Say someone cuts you up on the motorway; it can really shake you up. You might even start thinking, "What point was he trying to make? My driving's not so bad! What a bully!" Maybe it wasn't anything to do with you at all. You have no idea what goes on in other people's heads. Maybe the person who cut you up wasn't actually stupid, malicious or vile. They were probably just someone who was late, under a bit of stress, maybe unfamiliar with the road; there's any number of reasons. Have a little compassion, rather than immediate anger and condemnation.

Remember instead 'Hanlon's Razor.' It's a law that states: "Never attribute to malice that which is adequately explained by stupidity".

3. What's funny about this?

Sometimes, you just have to laugh. A few years ago, the airline JetBlue stranded its passengers on the runway for ten hours.

It took out adverts in the press to apologise profusely. Then the same thing happened to us a few days later! We were stuck on the runway at John F. Kennedy and had no choice but to laugh it off. Better to find humour in the situation than to feel helpless, or to get angry (as many did) with the poor flight attendants, who had no control over the situation either.

4. Will this matter one year from now?

Most of the time, whatever troubles us, isn't life-changing anyway. If it won't matter a year, month or even a day from now, why let it bother us at all?

5. What can I learn from this?

A life without problems is a life without personal growth. We believe that what determines the quality of our life, long-term, is our character. Napoleon Hill said that "every adversity, every failure, every heartache carries with it the seed on an equal or greater benefit."

6. Take yourself outside the problem

It's easy to give advice to others. We're outside their situation, so we can clearly see the alternative routes open to them, but when you're in the middle of a problem, suddenly our insight deserts us. We're eager to dish out our advice to other people, but when we're the ones in trouble, we're less keen to receive others' wisdom. Next time you're in a difficult situation, ask yourself how you'd advise a friend who was in a similar situation.

7. How else could I respond to this?

You might think you'd always give the same reaction, but that's probably not true. Imagine you're driving in a supermarket car park when someone backs out of their space and nearly hits you. You'd probably hoot your horn. Maybe you'd also react by swearing, shouting, or with a choice hand gesture.

But what if the same thing happened in a different location? This time, you're nearly home, driving down your road, when your neighbour backs out of his drive and, again, nearly hits you. Would you respond as aggressively towards him - shouting abuse or gesturing - or would you feel more able to laugh it off, once you'd both realised that no damage had been done?

You choose how you react in every situation; it's just that sometimes it's easy to forget that you really do have a choice. If it's not important, forget it and move on.

always look on the bright side of life

Monty Python

Key No.36: Accentuate the Positive

Let's look at how most people start a new health regime. Firstly, diet. They look at all the things they enjoy - maybe drinking, eating chocolate - and vow never to do them again (or at least, not until they've lost three stone, run their first marathon, or some other daunting goal).

Secondly, the fitness programme. They come up with a crushing schedule ("I'm going to join a gym and go five times a week!"), and resolve to do lots of activities that they actually dread. No wonder so many people give up on their fitness goals. In fact, it makes you wonder how anyone manages to achieve them with that mindset.

Make your vows positive ones. Aim to eat healthier foods, rather than swearing to give up cake forever. Focus on moving about more, rather than coming up with an iron-clad exercise schedule that terrifies you. That way, if you miss a day, you can shrug it off and keep going, rather than feeling like a failure.

**Focus on things you can achieve,
rather than setting yourself challenges
that will be difficult and
unpleasant to fulfil.**

Key No.37: Go With Your Gut

Do you believe in love at first sight? A good friend of Bobby's married her husband after dating him for only three weeks! At the time, people thought they were crazy. Fifteen years, three kids and one dog later, they're still in love.

Bobby once asked her how she could possibly have made such a decision after just three weeks. She said, "You just know." She went on her gut instinct.

Have you ever wondered how we make those snap decisions? The author Malcolm Gladwell explains, in his book *Blink*, that intuition is the result of a thought process so quick that we don't even realise we're doing it. So, can we really trust our gut with life-altering decisions?

Turns out that our gut and our brain really do work together! The vagus (the Latin for 'wandering') nerve is, at two feet long, the longest nerve in the body. It emerges from the brainstem, travels down the cervical spine, runs along the jugular vein, and then ends in the abdomen. It's the link between the Central Nervous System (CNS) in the brain, and the Enteric Nervous System (ENS) in the gastrointestinal system.

In the brain, it connects the areas that affect:

- Rate of respiration
- Bowel function
- Appetite
- Mood
- Seizures
- Emotions, such as anxiety
- Memory

There's increasing evidence showing that the vagus nerve is more than simply a relay station of receptors and transmitters; it acts as a complex and highly integrated 'brain' in its own right.

At the embryo stage, both our gut and our brain originate from the same mass of tissue. It divides during foetal development. One part develops into the CNS, and the other becomes the ENS. Later in the developmental process, the vagus nerve grows to connect the two nervous systems.

There's strong evidence linking the functions of the bowels with the functions of the brain. It might sound strange, but memories really are stored in the gut. You really do get gut feelings! Furthermore, our guts may have a significant effect on our mood.

Dr. Emeran Mayer MD is a gastroenterologist and the chairman of the new Mind-Body Collaborative Research Centre at the University of California. Dr Mayer describes the vagus nerve as a large electrical cable linking the brain and the digestive system. He states, "Doctors once believed the nerve's main job was controlling acid production in the stomach, [...] but 95 percent of the fibres go the other direction, from the gut to the brain."

That means that the health and function of our gut affects not just our brain function, but our psychological health as well. Here's how it works: the ENS is located in sheaths of tissue that line the oesophagus, stomach, small intestine and colon. It contains a dense network of neurons, neurotransmitters and proteins that relay messages between the neurons. It has a complex circuitry that enables it to learn, remember and produce what we've come to call 'gut feelings.'

Dr. Michael Gershon, Professor of Anatomy and Cell Biology at Columbia-Presbyterian Medical Center in New York City, identifies the entire gastrointestinal system as the body's secondary nervous system in his book, *The Second Brain*. "The brain is not the only place in the body that's full of neurotransmitters [... A] hundred million neurotransmitters line the length of the gut, approximately the same number found in the brain…"

Research indicates that almost every chemical, hormone and neurotransmitter that regulates the function of the brain, has been identified in the gut. When you next have a gut feeling, be sure to include it in your decision-making process, and examine it alongside all the relevant facts. Ask yourself the following three questions:

- "If I act on my intuition, what is the worst thing that could happen?"

- "…and what's the best thing that could happen?"

- "If I fail to act on my intuition, what opportunities might I miss?"

If there's no significant consequences in acting on your intuition - but you might lose an opportunity if you don't act - then go for it! The more you act on your intuition, the more you'll improve at analysing situations, so you'll be better able to act decisively and more effectively.

Next time you get a 'gut feeling' about an opportunity in your life or work, don't dismiss it out of hand. Instead, ask yourself, "What is my intuition trying to tell me?"

Key No.38: Talent Is Overrated

What do you reckon the number one ingredient for success is? Many people would say talent, but that's not the whole picture.

Take someone like Madonna. She's the highest selling female recording artist of all time, yet she's certainly not the best singer of all time. There are plenty of others with better vocal ability than her. So if it's not her singing ability that's made her the world's top selling female singer, what is it? As well as being a musician, Madonna's branched out to become a children's author, an actress, a fashion designer and a film producer.

So, does Madonna really have world-beating talents in all those areas too, or is there more to success than talent alone?

Madonna's famed for continually reinventing both the style of her music and her personal appearance. She's also always made her own decisions and stuck to her opinions even when others disagree, and she's never been afraid to take risks.

When she was 20, she dropped out of college and moved to New York City to try to make it as a dancer: "It was the first time I'd ever taken a plane, the first time I'd ever gotten a taxi cab. I came here with $35 in my pocket. It was the bravest thing I'd ever done."

Through her work as a dancer, she joined a band, then signed a solo recording deal. She kept working at her songs until she was happy with them, even firing her old producer at one point. Her singles took off, and her iconic image - lace tops, fishnet stockings, bleached hair, and bracelets - became one of the main looks of the 1980s.

Madonna has never rested on her laurels. She has always worked incredibly hard and sought to work with the hottest musicians to keep her sound fresh and forward; and her image has been equally important to her too. I'm sure you can remember loads of Madonna's iconic looks throughout her career, from the *Blond Ambition* corset to the pink leotard for *Hung Up*.

So, if it's not talent alone that's responsible for Madonna's world-beating success, what is? Well, the two strongest themes in her career would seem to be courage and dedication.

The courage of her convictions, the courage to take risks, and the dedication to her career; traits that are a common thread with anyone who does anything with excellence.

How many people do you know who want to do extraordinary things through ordinary efforts? People who have the desire, the dream and even the talent, but lack the will? People who talk about what they could and should be doing, but never actually do anything to make their daydreams into reality.

Mediocrity is the acceptance of anything less than what you know you are capable of. Excellence will not co-exist with mediocrity. Excellence is not a part-time job, or even a full-time job. Excellence is a permanent state of mind and a continual effort.

We can't tell you how many times we've watched an industry leader talking onstage and then had someone say, "I want to do what that guy on stage does." The usual reply from us is something along the lines of, "Well, great, but do you want to go through what he went through to get there?"

Many people have mistaken beliefs about what it takes to achieve excellence. As Josh Billings, the 19th century humourist once quipped, "It ain't so much the things we don't know that get us into trouble. It's the things we know that just ain't so."

Of course, talent is important to success. When someone listens to Mozart's *Requiem*, stares in awe at the works of Michelangelo on the ceiling of the Sistine Chapel, or even cheers as Wayne Rooney scores yet another goal, they're all inspired by the talent they witness. But how many others throughout history have been born with a brilliant mind, a genius for music, incredible sporting prowess, yet they still came and left unnoticed, tip-toeing from the cradle to the grave without their talent being recognised?

The problem with believing that talent is the root of all success is that you wind up believing that you either have talent, or you don't. That can lead to two undesirable outcomes:

1. If you believe that you've 'got it' then you may get complacent. Professional athletes all have talent, no question. But so do the tens of thousands of other athletes competing for the same position. Talent is not enough; extraordinary performance demands extraordinary efforts directed at continual improvement.

2. If you feel that you don't have talent, then you'll probably never step up and even take a shot at getting what you want as you may feel that you just don't have it in you.

Both perspectives are misguided. The world is full of talented individuals who have potential but haven't managed to act on it, so they live in constant frustration, continually aware of the gap between who they are and who they are capable of being.

Admittedly, you probably know someone who maybe didn't have exceedingly high aptitude, but still became very good at what they do, and successful in their field. This possibility, though true, is an exception, not the people.

Another false belief is that people who are world class got there only through hard work. Surely, if hard work by itself was enough to guarantee success, then nurses would be among the wealthiest, most influential people in our society. Yet just about everyone, who's at the top of their field, appears to work very, very hard.

So, if it's not hard work that separates the top performer from the average performer, why do elite professionals work so hard? Well, yes, they do work hard, but they work quite differently to the average person who may be working long hours, but just not very effectively.

Many people mistake activity for productivity, and think that repetition improves performance. Merely engaging in the same tasks repeatedly won't increase your skill level, regardless of how many hours per day you work. Performance is only improved through mindful practise with intense focus and concentration.

Elite athletes, professionals and performers all understand the power of practise and mental rehearsal. They understand that it's not a question of effort, but results; and those results are dependent on how effectively the effort is applied.

There are four keys to effective practise:

Meta cognition

In simple terms, meta cognition is thinking about your thinking. All the top performers are fanatical about practiae. Athletes like Steven Gerrard are the best in their class because despite their innate talents, they devote hours per day engaging in intense, hard and focused practise. Excellence requires a clear mental picture of what ideal performance looks like, and they go through mental rehearsals in explicit detail. The more focused you are in practise, the more you will be in flow during your performance.

Feedback

Top performers practise with a plan. They're able to step back and observe the gap between their desired performance and their actual performance. They have the ability to ask themselves questions such as:

- What am I currently doing well, and in-line with my ideal performance?
- Where do I need to improve?
- How can I improve my level of performance?

Top performers always seek to improve themselves. This might be through formal coaching, but you'll often find that they engage in informal coaching as well. They'll surround themselves with colleagues and friends who possess equal or greater skill than they do. Elite performers seek out and accept constructive feedback, and then they act on it.

Continuity

Remember Malcolm Gladwell's assertion, in his book *Outliers*, that exceptional individuals didn't realise their full potential until they had practised for tens of thousands of hours? Top performers don't do their craft part-time or as a hobby. They don't even do it full-time, which is about 40 hours per week. The top performer thinks about their craft all the time and practises day in and out.

When you see a successful person perform, we often envy them their lifestyle and talent. But what we often don't see is the thousands and thousands of hours of work that got them there; the painstaking concentration and sacrifice that was made before there was ever any guarantee of achieving their goals.

Passion

Top performers are able to make extraordinary efforts because they love what they do. The process of becoming better is a reward in itself. So many people hold back because they make such a big deal about the effort required. They only think about the pain, sacrifice and potential failure they will have to endure, meaning that they never put in the effort required, so that their failure becomes a self-fulfilling prophecy.

Persistence and dedication are more important than talent. But practise carefully: practise doesn't make perfect; it makes permanent!

∼

Key No.39: Imagine It to Achieve It

In 1966, the American pilot Captain Gerald Coffee was shot down over Vietnam and taken into captivity. He was a Prisoner of War for seven years and, during that time, was deprived of everything we take for granted. He lived in a small, cold, dark, wet cell, in solitary confinement; conditions that have driven others insane.

Captain Coffee had no external stimulation, and was therefore forced to turn inwards to stave off boredom and potential madness. So, every day, he practised golf. He'd remember his favourite past-time vividly; he'd conjure up the wind on his face, smell the freshly cut grass, grip the golf club in his hand.

After his release, the Captain was keen to play golf again for real; and when he played his first game as a free man, it was the best game of his whole life. He outperformed himself, even though he hadn't actually played in seven years. When interviewed about his incredible achievement, he credited all the visualisation work that he'd done for his performance.

It's well known that professional athletes also use visualisation to enhance their performance in practise and in competition. One such athlete, whom Bobby has had the privilege and the pleasure of working with, is Sally Gunnell. In her day, Sally was a supreme track and field athlete, and the only female British athlete to have claimed gold in all four Olympic, World, European and Commonwealth Games.

In the lead up to winning the 400 m hurdles at the 1992 Barcelona Olympics and sprinting on to a new world record the following year at the World Championships in Stuttgart, Sally practised visualisation with such steadfast commitment and consistency that when she actually crossed the finish line in Stuttgart, she really didn't know whether it was real or her imagination!

Sally's mind was so focused on her outcome that she actually managed to blur the boundaries between what she visualised and what she actualised. Lucky for her, it was real and so were the gold medals she later received on the medal podiums!

However, both Sally Gunnell and Captain Coffee are exceptional people – one a highly trained athlete with incredible focus, the other a celebrated Naval Officer who received, during his career, the Silver Star, two Purple Hearts, two Bronze Stars, two awards of the Legion of Merit, just to name a few. It's not totally surprising that they would use visualisation so effectively. The question is, can it work just as effectively for an average person?

Doctors Guang Yue and Kelly Cole from the University of Iowa proved that it can. Their research, published in the *Journal of Neurophysiology* (Vol. 67, Issue 5, 1992), showed that a person can strengthen a muscle using only the power of imagination.

Yue and Cole took two groups of participants and told them to exercise a single finger. One of the groups did this by actually performing fifteen finger contractions at a time, with a 20-second period of rest between sets.

The other group was told to imagine that they were performing the same contractions, with the same rest period. They were also told to envision a voice shouting "Harder! Harder! Harder!" at them.

At the end of the study, those who'd actually performed the exercises increased the muscular strength of their finger by 30%. Amazingly, the group that simply imagined that they were performing the exercises increased their muscular strength by 22%!

This phenomenon is explained by Dr. Norman Doidge in his book *The Brain That Changes Itself*. He says: "During these imaginary contractions, the neurons responsible for stringing together sequences of instructions for movements are activated and strengthened, resulting in increased strength when the muscles are contracted."

Dr. Bruce Lipton backs up these findings in his book, *The Biology of Belief*, and states: "Thoughts, the minds' energy, directly influence how the brain controls the body's physiology."

When we imagine something, for example, an apple, the visual cortex in our brain processes that image in the same way as if we were actually looking at an apple. The more vividly you imagine, the more senses you involve and the more regions of your brain become active. For example, if you see the apple clearly in your mind and can taste its sweetness as well, you've activated the 'Primary Gustatory Regions' of your brain.

Here are four more great reasons to use visualisation regularly:

1. When you visualise, you're forced to focus on the job at hand. This means that you have to give it your full attention, rather than letting the minutiae of daily life (what to have for supper, whether you need more milk) distract you.

2. When you're concentrating on the results, and the ensuring benefits that you want to produce, you're not thinking about the things in your life that cause you stress. So visualisation can actually help you turn 'work' into a bit of escapism.

3. It gives you a feeling of control over your performance, which in turn will give you greater confidence and self-assurance in the related task.

4. Not only will your performance improve, it will also become more consistent.

Our minds really can't tell the difference between what's vividly imagined and what's occurring in reality. Use the power of visualisation to improve your performance!

~

Key No.40: Failure Is Inevitable, Defeat Is Not

"Whoever tries the most stuff and screws the most stuff up and most rapidly launches the next try wins. Failures are not to be 'tolerated,' they are to be celebrated."

- Tom Peters, business expert and author.

B obby once spoke at a conference in Whistler, Canada. Just after he'd finished his talk, a delegate approached him and asked, "How do I apply all that correctly, without making a mistake?"

Why are people obsessed with not slipping up? Excellence is a process of continuous learning, and learning is the continuous process of trial and error. Whoever coined the phrase, "If you're going to do something, do it right the first time," probably never did anything else significant in his entire life.

The road to excellence is paved with 'failures.' Take Thomas Edison. In 1878, Joseph Swan received a British patent for the invention of the electric light bulb. Edison, who was at the time one of the most prolific inventors in the world (holding 1,093 patents in the US alone and many others abroad), saw an opportunity to increase the commercial potential of Swan's invention by creating a filament that would burn significantly longer.

Edison had a reputation for many things. If you had asked Joseph Swan, maybe he'd have called him an arrogant, credit-seeking thief. Perhaps the inventor Nikola Tesla would have agreed.

To others, however, he was also one of the most prolific inventors in the world.

For a whole year, Edison worked tirelessly, often going days with barely any sleep. In that one year, he reportedly planned, executed and scrutinised over 10,000 prototype light bulbs. Then, on October 22nd, 1879, he completed his first successful test of the carbon filament incandescent light. On January 27th, 1880, he was awarded US patent 223,898.

When asked why he'd persisted in his experiments despite having failed over 10,000 times, Edison remarked that he never once failed. Instead, he believed that he had discovered over 10,000 ways not to invent the light bulb!

Maybe Edison sounds delusional and unrealistic, but he took our homes out of an age of candlelight and into a new world of electricity.

He simply realised something that others didn't: failure is a single isolated event, not a person. He didn't get caught up in the emotion. Instead, he viewed each result simply as that, a result. Each experiment gave him feedback to adjust his methods, and then to try again with new insight.

Similarly, when Thomas J. Watson, founder of IBM, was asked the secret to success, he replied, "Double your rate of failure."

Many of us are afraid to try because we risk failure. Failure is inevitable, defeat is not. We somehow mistakenly believe that an outcome is a reflection on us, rather than an opportunity to re-evaluate what we're doing. We become paralysed with fear over a result that hasn't even occurred yet. If we do manage to get ourselves going, we perform far below our potential because our fear has heightened the activity of our amygdala; this robs glucose from our prefrontal lobes, in turn decreasing our critical thinking skills and reducing our mental faculties. Basically, when we fear failure, it virtually guarantees that we'll produce exactly those results. Failure is a self-fulfilling prophecy.

"Far better is it to dare mighty things, to win glorious triumphs, even though checkered by failure... than to rank with those poor spirits who neither enjoy nor suffer much, because they live in a Gray twilight that knows not victory nor defeat."
- Theodore Roosevelt

If we can stop ourselves from becoming overwhelmed with emotion over our results and relinquish our need for control, we can accept that a 'bad' outcome is often just as profitable as a 'good' outcome.

When things go well, we rejoice, and when they don't, we reflect. Very often wisdom is the result of experience (usually an unpleasant one) and reflection.

Acquiring knowledge is a process;
we need to apply what we've learnt
in a way that's meaningful.
So, each so-called failure
will be incredibly useful
when we take the time to reflect on it;
it will take us one step closer
to the wisdom that will enable us
to ultimately succeed.

~

Key No.41: Don't Be A Lame Duck

One sweltering summer morning, Pete was commuting on the Tube. Usually, he'd just bury his head in the paper, but on this particular day, he decided to look up and observe what was going on all around.

The heat in the carriage was stifling. Sitting or standing, his fellow travellers were blank faced and emotionless. It may as well have been a carriage full of mannequins. Then, the train ground to a halt in the middle of the tunnel, with no apparent explanation.

Eventually, a voice crackled over the loud speaker, informing the passengers that they had stopped due to a sick passenger at West Ham. Pete looked at the other passengers. Curiously, there was virtually no reaction from anyone. Just the consistent look of passive despondency.

Dr. Stefan Klein says, "Despondency is a product of resignation." This particular morning, Pete wondered, after doing the same commute to work every morning, day after day, year after year, how many of his fellow passengers had just given up and didn't care anymore?

In 1965, the psychologist Dr. Martin Seligman conducted an experiment at the University of Pennsylvania. He placed two groups of dogs into two separate boxes, rigged with an electric current. He gave low-level electrical shocks to both groups of dogs. In the first group, the dogs could stop the shocks by simply pressing their noses on a lever in the box. The second group of dogs had no means of halting the pain.

In the second phase of the experiment, all of the dogs were transferred to different boxes that were similarly rigged with an electric current. These new boxes were so shallow that the dogs could easily jump out of the box and avoid the pain. The first group of dogs, who'd been able to end the shocks by pressing the lever, simply stepped out of the box and walked away. The second lot of dogs (those who hadn't been able to stop the shocks the first time) just sat there whimpering and making no attempt to avoid their pain, although they easily could have walked away. Eventually, these dogs demonstrated a reduction in their basic biological drives, losing the motivation for food, activity and sex. Dr. Seligman termed this conditioned response as 'learned helplessness.'

Whether it's our feeling of powerlessness over being stuck in a train carriage or the lack of control we have over the progression of our career, or the continued failure to lose weight, these circumstances all affect us. When we frequently experience a situation that seems out of our control, we become conditioned by it. Humans, as with the dogs, can easily succumb to learned helplessness.

Brain imaging shows clearly that feelings of powerlessness lead to a decreased activity in the left prefrontal cortex. This region of the brain affects drive and emotional control. The net effect of feeling powerless is a reduction in our ability to experience emotion, resulting in a level of pervasive depression.

Everyone experiences disappointment and frustration. It's not necessarily a bad thing. If we stop and reflect on the source of our disappointment, then take action to change our methods and circumstances, it can be very constructive. However, when we're constantly exposed to triggers that make us suffer disappointment day after day, it conditions us and ultimately alters our brain's biochemistry.

To be clear, adverse emotional states are normal responses to traumatic events in our lives, such as the loss of a loved one. Prolonged trauma, however, will eventually re-programme our brains so that our depression isn't the result of the trauma anymore, but instead it's the result of our new brain chemistry. Our levels of the stress hormone norepinephrine become imbalanced as our serotonin levels drop. When coupled with an increase in cortisol, this adversely affects everything from sex drive, motivation, aggression, to sleep and overall mood.

According to a report in the June 15th, 1999 edition of the *Journal of Neuroscience*, MRIs indicated that otherwise healthy women with a history of depression have smaller hippocampal structures. The hippocampus plays an integral role in memory and learning. This means that learned helplessness doesn't just mean the loss of our drive, it also can mean the loss of ourselves.

Our emotional state, and therefore, the level of our performance, isn't based upon the reality of our situation, but rather on the meaning we attach to it.

Unfortunately, some people come to see the world through a distorted filter; their world view no longer influences the environment in their brain, instead the environment in their brain dictates their world view.

Surely you know someone who's met repeated failure, and who greets every challenge and every suggestion with a declaration, like "I've tried that already, it won't work".

It doesn't work? Ever? For anyone at any time? Of course, it does; it just didn't work for them. They felt disappointed, which altered the chemistry in their brain, and then they continued to think about that disappointment day after day, until they altered their brain chemistry permanently.

It's a vicious circle; they feel powerless, which alters their brain, and those alterations decrease their motivation to change, which in turn increases their perception of powerlessness. Happily, learnt helplessness can also be unlearned. Just as continuous conditioning can create it, daily conditioning can break it.

When we work with clients who feel truly helpless and frustrated, we have a special programme to help them towards recovery. The first step is to help them gather evidence proving to themselves that they're actually achievers that are successful in many aspects of life.

Try this daily exercise. Every day, write down three things that you've accomplished, no matter how big or small. For example, going for a walk, doing your paperwork, or even just making your bed!

When you realise that there are many things in your day that you can, and do, achieve, you'll start to see yourself differently. When you see yourself in a better light, you'll begin to notice other possibilities. When you start focusing on how you can act in a given situation, you'll start affecting your brain chemistry positively. In the same way that continual negative duck talk conditions your brain, so does applied continual positive thought. You'll start seeing solutions to your problems, rather than concentrating on the seeming hopelessness of a situation.

Starting with a seemingly trivial action can lead to an outcome that once seemed impossible.

**As the philosopher Lao Tzu said,
"A journey of a thousand miles
begins with a single step."**

∾

Key No.42: Just 'Cause It walks Like a Duck, Doesn't Mean It's a Duck

One hot, humid morning, Bobby went for a walk along the promenade in Brighton, a town just outside London. He noticed a hunched figure creeping along, an old man struggling with four shopping bags.

Even with a cane, he could barely walk. Every few steps, he would have to stop and catch his breath before painfully resuming his pitifully slow walk. Bobby continues the story below:

"I really felt for the man. It was blisteringly hot, and sweat was running down my face just from taking a gentle stroll. I couldn't imagine how this old man felt, but I was sure he would appreciate help.

"When I caught up with him, I asked him how far he was going and asked if he would mind if I carried his bags a bit. He looked at me like I was crazy and asked, 'What do you want with me?' When I took his bags, he barked, 'I don't want anyone walking with me, I don't like company. Can't understand why you want to carry my bloody bags anyway. What's the matter with you?'

"We walked along together. For the first 10 minutes, Joe was silent. Then, he started talking to me. Turns out that he was on the European Front in World War II. He had moved to Brighton in 1956. Some ten years after that, he lost his first wife. He later remarried. This time to a lady who was a smoker. Joe hated smoking, so his wife quit. Unfortunately not soon enough; she died shortly after she was diagnosed with lung cancer.

"We discussed our mutual love of Cornish Pasties, agreeing that a pastry filled case, baked with beef, turnips, tomato and onion, are nothing short of genius. We couldn't agree on whether its origins are actually Cornish or, as rumour has it, Devon. In any case, they're delicious and Joe, and I, rather like them.

"As we talked, Joe revealed he quite enjoyed the cinema, and that he watches films all the time these days, because he's alone and has been for some time now. At the end of our walk, he offered to buy me a cup of tea. He said that he wished he could see me again whenever I came back to Brighton. He seemed genuinely grateful for the conversation, as well as sad to see me go. I left Joe in front of his house.

"As I walked on, I couldn't get the words, 'I am all alone now,' out of my head. For such an initially 'grumpy old man', he was so pleasant to talk to. He wasn't as much a grumpy old man, as he was a lonely old man. He had lost everyone who mattered to him. Initiating a relationship, even with someone who just wanted to help with his bags, is painful for him. So, my first impression of him was quite wrong. In different circumstances, I might have completely misjudged him and lost the opportunity to connect with him.

"Later that day, I couldn't help thinking how this echoed so many encounters I have had with so many other people throughout my life. Even with the best intentions, sometimes, the response we get from others is less than encouraging.

"Luckily, sometimes, we're able to realise over time that the people who seem most hurtful are, in reality, those who are hurting most. Often, these are the people who actually want and need us the most. They just think that they have too much to lose. They require the reassurance that they're safe with us emotionally before they can trust us.

"Even if we do our best to ignore them, our judgements are still likely to be expressed through the tone of our voice and through non-verbal communication (e.g. body language, facial expression). Earlier in this chapter, we mentioned that some people need to feel a level of safety and acceptance before they can communicate with us.

"When we express our deeply held prejudices, whether consciously or subconsciously, we risk making these people feel uncomfortable, thereby preventing them from connecting with us. This, in turn, reduces our level of effectiveness.

"Regardless of our initial encounter, my first impression of Joe was wrong. In truth, despite being from completely different generations, Joe and I had many similarities and were able to make a good connection."

When you meet someone for the first time, ask yourself the following questions. You may also wish to try these questions on your existing friendships and acquaintances too. The answers may surprise you:

1. What do I like about this person? (The greater our affinity, the greater the possibility of empathising.)

2. What do I have in common with this person? (The greater the common ground, the less potential for stigmatisation.)

3. What question can I use to help this person arrive at his or her own conclusions? (If we hold another person in less than unconditional positive regard, then our "well meaning" advice may be perceived as criticism. When we ask questions, we help the other person arrive at their own conclusions by creating greater self-accountability; directing more focus toward the other person and opening up the possibility for greater understanding on both sides.)

Don't rush to conclusions about other people. When you scratch their surface, you might be surprised by what you actually find. We're all imperfect, and that gives us the common ground we need in order to communicate with empathy and help others change.

Prejudice is a burden that confuses the past, threatens the future and renders the present inaccessible.

Maya angelou

Key No.43: You Can Rewire Your Brain

There are simple solutions to the everyday problems we face. For example, do you want to lose weight? Then simply eat less and exercise more. Want to give up smoking? Don't light another cigarette. Tired? Get more sleep!

It all sounds so easy, doesn't it? So why do we find it so hard to change? It's not because the solutions are difficult (they're obviously not) and it's not because we don't have the willpower. The reason why most people find it hard to change is because of the way our brain form habits.

Our brain sometimes work in a primitive way; one of the things it's designed to do is learn new behaviours to the point where they become automatic. This means you can do things like brush your teeth and tie your shoelaces without having to think, every single time, about how to do them. We need actions we do frequently to be automatic so that our attention and energy can be directed to other things.

Our ability to form habits is really useful if the habits are ones we want. Unfortunately, many of us have habits we no longer want or need. Take a moment to think of things that your brain does automatically that you don't want it to do. Maybe you worry unnecessarily, comfort eat, give yourself a hard time, bite your nails, or drink too much? They're all destructive habits, and you can probably think of plenty more.

The reason that we have both helpful and unhelpful habits is because your brain doesn't know the difference between those that are useful to you and those that aren't. The easiest thing for the brain to do is what it's done before; unless you train it to do otherwise, it will happily keep on doing what it's always done.

Neuroscientists have confirmed that when we learn to do something, we form new connections in our brain that reinforce our behaviour: this is called 'plasticity'. It means that the brain is not hardwired and new circuits can be formed that override older ones. This means it's never too late to change your behaviour. You might think that you're set in your ways, but no matter how old you are, or how long you've been doing something, you can change if you want to.

'We are what we repeatedly do.
Excellence, then, is not an act,
but a habit.'

- Aristotle

Here's an exercise which will show you how easy it can be to reprogramme your brain. Read through the following paragraph, then put the book down and try it.

Cross your arms as you usually would. Notice which arm is on top. How does this feel? Probably quite comfortable and normal. Now uncross your arms and fold them the other way (i.e. if you're right arm was on top the first time, fold your arms so the left is on top.) Notice how this feels.

Probably quite strange or even quite uncomfortable? Now, cross your arms again, so they're back as you'd normally fold them. Notice how comforting it feels, returning to your old way. Now cross and uncross your arms 21 times – each time putting a different arm on top. Compare how it feels to have each arm on top. Is there such a big difference now between the top arms?

Some people find that after doing this exercise once, they notice a big difference in how they feel. Other people need to do it a few more times, or for a couple of minutes every day, before they start to feel comfortable. Whatever your experience, we guarantee that if you do this exercise every day, after a while, it would feel normal to fold your arms either way.

That's a simple example of how your brain can learn to do something new. It just requires repetition, a willingness to feel a little discomfort for a while, and a sense of adventure. Play around with your life. See how it would feel if you slept on the other side of the bed, if you swapped your knife and fork between your hands, or moved your mouse with your other hand. Chances are it would feel a little bit strange and uncomfortable, at first, until you got used to it.

Habits are just things that you do. They can be broken. You can retrain your brain until the new behaviour feels natural.

Key No.44: Your Happiness Is Your Responsibility

How old is the study of happiness? You may well think it's a pretty recent thing, but, over 2,300 years ago, there was a Chinese philosopher called Mencius who talked of happiness. He believed that the more joy we find in doing things - simple things, like chatting with a neighbour, cooking meals or harvesting rice - the more motivated we are.

Zhuangzi was a contemporary of Mencius, and he claimed that a sense of humour was essential to happiness. He believed that when we laugh, we stop being rational. By freeing ourselves from rational thought, we are able to go along with things as they are, rather than feeling pressure to do or have more.

I wonder what he would have thought about our world today; how so many people are motivated only by personal or financial gain, and how seriously many people take themselves.

Buddha is revered as one of the greatest philosophers who ever lived. He believed that the cause of unhappiness is craving, which he called "mental dysfunction" or "dukkha". You can see how true that is for so many of us today. We crave more money, beauty, possessions, attention, and love. However much we have, we still want more. Nothing can ever satisfy our hunger.

Aristotle had a similar view of happiness, teaching that we had to depend on ourselves for happiness. He actually saw happiness as the central purpose of human life and a goal in itself. Dr. Gregory Berns of Emory University has an intriguing twist on the various theories of happiness. He sees happiness as a passive emotion, something that comes to us rather than something we can obtain directly.

Instead of happiness, he believes that he should pursue satisfaction. Satisfaction comes from experiencing new things, and from being motivated to do something that has personal significance. When we commit to something that someone else wants us to do, or that society deems valuable, Berns claims that we should look for our own meaning and purpose in the task, otherwise it won't be satisfying.

Do not expect other people or possessions to make you happy. Happiness comes from within. Appreciate what you have and see the beauty in the small moments in life.

Key No.45: If You Want Roses, Plant Them!

The poet George Eliot said that "It will never rain roses: when we want to have more roses, we must plant more [rose] trees."

It's easy to want something. It's another thing entirely to be prepared to work to achieve it. Many people want to get fit, but won't actually put in the necessary work to change themselves. Or, they'll dream of a new career, but refuse to actually study or do anything that will take them closer to their dream job.

Sophie, a good friend of mine, lost over 50 pounds in 18 months. She recalled an old pal greeting her with amazement: "Wow, what's your secret? I need to lose some weight myself!" Sophie then explained that there wasn't a secret as such; it boiled down to eating less and exercising more. At this, her pal's face fell. "Oh!" she exclaimed, "But that sounds like hard work!"

If something's worth achieving, it's worth working at. You need to invest time, energy and commitment into your goals, and you need to expect a few knocks along the way. You're never going to get your roses otherwise.

Malcolm Gladwell's book *Outliers* is a fascinating look at high achievers in all walks of life. He asserts that elite performance comes from around 10,000 hours of practise, and quotes the neurologist Dr. Daniel Levitin: "[It appears]... that ten thousand hours of practice is required to achieve the level of mastery associated with being a world-class expert – in anything. In study after study, of composers, basketball players, fiction writers, ice skaters, concert pianists, chess players, master criminals, and what have you, this number comes up again and again."

And it's obvious, isn't it? The harder you work at something, the better you get at it?

But so many people feel that they're somehow entitled to a level of success, without having to put the work in. They begrudge others their achievements. Take the old joke: How many actors does it take to change a light bulb? Five! One to climb the ladder and the other four to say, "That should be me up there!"

There does seem to be a problem in today's society with feelings of entitlement. If you feel that there's a big gap between what you have and what you 'deserve,' there's going to be a big obstacle to finding happiness.

It's easy to look at someone's success (the end result) and ignore the work that lead to it: the tens of thousands of hours spent practising, the tens of thousands of pounds, euros, and dollars spent on advanced education, and the many failures endured along the way.

Sure, some people do just get lucky and get presented with an opportunity that far exceeds their actual competency; but that's the exception.

Don't be disheartened if you don't get the results you want right away, whether it's at work, or in a fitness programme, or in learning a new hobby. Don't assume you're not smart enough, or that you don't have the potential. Instead, consider that it's probably because you haven't put in enough time or effort yet.

Anything worth achieving takes sacrifice, enormous effort, humility, perseverance, not to mention a bit of patience with yourself. As the film producer Samuel Goldwyn said: "The harder I work, the luckier I get."

~

Key No.46: Don't Keep Up With the Joneses

Most of us want to fit in and be accepted by those around us, and this makes us happy because we feel like we belong. So, we fit in by choosing to wear the same clothes, live in the same area, drive similar cars and go on holiday to the same places as our friends, family and peers. That's fine, to a certain extent; but this 'keeping up with the Joneses' can be a problem if it gets out of hand.

There is always more to want; bigger houses, faster cars, more expensive clothes to buy. As we've already discussed, this means than instead of enjoying what we have now, we find ourselves dreaming about our future purchases and achievements. Eventually, we feel disappointed with the things we already have.

Unfortunately, many of us have lost touch with what is 'normal' in terms of money, looks and lifestyle. The media tends to glorify actors, musicians, presenters, and even people who are famous for just being famous. That means we're often presented with images of 'normality' that frankly aren't actually normal, but still filters into our subconscious.

Realistically, we know these stars don't roll out of bed looking perfectly preened. An army of stylists, hairdressers, make-up artists, photographers and digital retouchers see to that. In many cases, a plastic surgeon can take a large chunk of the credit, but, that doesn't stop many 'ordinary' people from comparing themselves to those unrealistic images and hating what they see in the mirror. Many of those people then go to extremes to try to change themselves; going under the knife to change their noses, enlarge their breasts, slim their thighs with painful liposuction. They'll spend money that they don't have on new clothes, expensive haircuts, and the latest must-have miracle beauty product. According to Credit Action, a UK charity that educates people about money to help them avoid getting into debt, the amount of personal debt in the UK increases by £1 million every five minutes and the total amount of personal debt in the UK at the end of June 2008 stood at £1.444 billion.

In his book *Affluenza*, the psychologist Oliver James writes that two-thirds of Britons believe that they cannot afford everything they really need. Even when their earnings increase, they still believe that they can't have everything; this leads to anxiety and depression. We tell ourselves the next promotion, or maybe a sudden windfall, would make us happier. Note that these are external thing. We're refusing to take charge of our own happiness and hoping that something happens to make us happy.

Oliver James said: "We have become absolutely obsessed with measuring ourselves and others through the distorted lens of affluenza values... the great majority of people now define their lives through earnings, possessions, appearances and celebrity and those things are making them miserable because they impede the meeting of our fundamental needs."

**Remember that there are real people behind the celebrities, but they're often buried under many layers of make-up, PhotoShop and, often, misery.
Don't compare yourself to anyone else;
just concentrate on appreciating
what you have right now.**

Key No.47: Life Isn't a Dress Rehearsal

I'm always amazed by how many people believe that there is nothing they can do to change their lives. I hope by now you realise that you can change anything you want! To help you focus your efforts, work through the following exercise:

Imagine that you're 99 years old and looking back over your life. Ask yourself:

- What do you wish you had done less of? Write down two or three things here. Examples could include being less critical, worrying less, not working as hard, or procrastinating less often.

- What do you wish you had done more of? Write down some of these things. Examples might be relaxing more, travelling to new places, spending more time with family and friends, laughing more, and having more fun.

Well, here comes the great news: chances are you're not 99 yet! So, if you had any regrets when you were doing this exercise, you can start taking steps now to make sure they don't become reality.

Look at the list of things you wish you'd done more of. If these are things you really want to do, make time to do them. Then look at the list of what you wish you'd done less of. What's stopping you from changing them? Again, it's not too late to stop doing these things.

**You can decide to do
whatever you want.
It's never too late
to change your life!**

∽

Key No.48: There's Nothing to Fear

**"The experience of overcoming fear
is extraordinarily delightful."**

- Bertrand Russell

Arguably, as a baby, you only knew unlimited possibility. You could become anyone, go anywhere, or do anything. You didn't know that you could, but equally you didn't know that you couldn't. You didn't know the difference between good and bad, right and wrong, positive or negative. You didn't understand trust, guilt or values.

Instead, you just did exactly what you wanted to do, when you wanted to do it, on your own terms. You slept. You cried because you were hungry, or because you needed to be held, or because you needed your nappy changed. When offered milk, you'd drink only if you felt like it. You were in control of your own universe. In fact, you thought you were the universe.

Gradually, you started learning that the world actually consists of not just you, but objects and other people too. Your mother became very important in your life, because she provided you with food, warmth and love.

As you grew, your understanding of the world continued to change. New rules arrived, telling you how to behave and what you shouldn't do. You discovered that you weren't fine how you were, after all.

Your parents wanted to mould you, to prepare you in the best way they thought possible for the world. They thought it would be easier for you if you were like other people. They insisted that they wanted you to be like them. You had to eat when and what they wanted to eat.

Maybe you resented this, and for a time, you certainly fought against it, but as demands were continually placed on you, you learnt how to be obedient, to comply or conform to a way that was alien to you at the time, but became second nature to you with practise.

In your babyhood, you didn't have problems or fears. But by the time you started school, you had already been exposed to attitudes and values that influenced the way you thought and acted. As you grew older, you absorbed most of your beliefs second-hand; your family, culture, religion, and education all shaped how you act and react. You learnt to distrust your own senses and, in many cases, became frightened of being yourself.

Chances are you moved into adult life believing that, deep down, you were flawed in some way. If you have this notion that you are not good enough, you are certainly going to be frightened.

Most people believe that showing fear or being frightened is a weakness. Many people go to crazy lengths to pretend to themselves that they're not frightened, but the fear will always manifest itself in some way. Fear can make people ill, develop allergies, or come up with apparently logical reasons for following a regrettable course of behaviour; all this to hide the fact that, deep down, they are scared.

If your life is ruled by unwelcome fears, you are wasting a lot of your time and energy. Fear is often about trying to deal with the future before it arrives. Obviously, that's impossible because we can't always predict what lies ahead. We can't control the future by worrying about it. Equally, you can't change the past by endlessly criticising and judging yourself, and others, for things that happened.

Nothing in life is fixed. Anything can happen, at any time. This can be really exciting if you have lots of confidence in yourself; but if you haven't, it can feel very frightening.

Although you cannot control the world around you, you can learn to control your own fearful reactions, and in the process find serenity and happiness.

One of the best things about the past is that it's over. There's a much better place to focus your attention: the present. Don't waste your time being frightened about things that could happen, might happen or may never happen.

The future is right here, right now. The only thing you have control of is this moment. Not tomorrow, not next week, not next year. Just now.

This very moment is fresh and new. You can do whatever you want with it; you've got as much control over it as you dare to give yourself.

To conquer your fear, you must first understand it and know how to deal with it when it affects you. It may take some time to rewrite the past, but the reward will be worth it.

Fear can be useful. It's an integral part of our make-up. Our distant ancestors needed fear for their survival. If there was a sabre-toothed tiger stalking them, they needed to be able to get away, fast. Having no fear at all can be deadly. Babies and toddlers don't understand the danger of water, or traffic, or heights. They require constant supervision because their fearless nature can very easily prove fatal.

When our brains wire up in our very early years, a fear reflex kicks in. If we trip or hurt ourselves, we release the hormone adrenaline. Soon, this fight-or-flight chemical can be triggered by the suggestion that we might be about to hurt ourselves. A surge of this chemical gives us the focus and strength to remove ourselves from a potentially dangerous situation. For example, many people get nervous when a dog barks because they assume that the dog could potentially attack. It's probably a very friendly dog, just a loud one, but the fear takes over and the rational brain shuts off.

Fear gives you an adrenaline surge. From a small dose that gives you butterflies in the stomach, to a powerful dose that makes your heart jump and forces you to flee.

While fear can be essential, in many situations, it merely holds you back from reaching your potential.

But many people never make the effort to overcome their minor fears because they're creatures of comfort. We formulate ways of thinking and acting, which become habits, even when we'd be better off doing something else.

You may find the idea of change uncomfortable, even if change leads to getting rid of the pain and discomfort that your fear causes you; but once you are committed to approaching things in a different way, change is possible.

An old farmer had ploughed around a large rock in one of his fields for years. He had broken several ploughshares on it and had even grown rather superstitious about the rock. After breaking yet another piece of equipment on it, he finally decided to do something about it. When he put a crowbar under the rock, he discovered that it was only about six inches thick, and that he could break it up easily with a sledgehammer! As he was carting the pieces away, he reflected on all the trouble that the rock had caused him over the years, and how easy it would have been to have got rid of it sooner.

Think about your fear for a few moments as if it were that rock. Is your fear getting in the way of your life? Though you may have had your fear for a long time, it doesn't mean that you cannot remove it. It may even be much easier than you thought.

The key is in breaking the way you think about your fear and choosing to respond differently.

We've worked with people in the past who kept talking over and over about their problems, without actually doing anything about them. They felt better for talking about their worries (and there's nothing wrong with talking about them), but if they only talk and don't actually do anything about them, those issues will never go away.

In order to start tackling your fears, you need to get into the habit of experiencing change.

**"Anxiety and fear produce energy.
Where we focus that energy noticeably
affects the quality of our lives:
Focus on the solution,
not the problem."**

- Walter Anderson

Get used to the idea of change. Start by doing as many things differently as you can. Take a different route to work, sleep on the other side of the bed, buy something you wouldn't normally eat next time you're in the supermarket. Tackling these little tasks will give you the confidence that you really can change. Eventually, you'll naturally start tackling the bigger areas in your life. All you have to do is break down your big fear into little challenges that you can easily manage.

Take control of your fear, and don't let it determine which paths you follow in life. Once you start examining your fears, you may be surprised at how shallow they really are!

Key No.49: Look to the Sky

The Chinese have always known about the importance of nature and what they term the elements: earth, fire, air, wood, water. The only reason we are all on this Earth is because of these ancient elements. Remove one of them, and there is no life. When Pete went to China, he noticed (whatever time of day it was) that people everywhere practised the ancient martial art of T'ai Chi. It's a fine tradition of people energising themselves by exercising outdoors, in the elements.

One of the best ways to restore and nourish your soul is to find time to go outside, look around, and be with nature.

We need natural relaxation in our lives. Whether it's looking at a beautiful view, lying in a hot bath, reading a book, or relaxing in a hammock.

There was an ingenious study of depression. The psychologist told the subjects, who were all despondent, that they had two weeks to prepare for their depression therapy. For those two weeks, he wanted them to go out every day and see how many chimneys they could find. Why chimneys?

Well, it's a brilliant bit of thinking. People who are frightened, depressed and worried tend to look downwards and inwards. That's because they indulge in a lot of self-analysis, so the psychologist was forcing them to look upwards and outwards.

After two weeks, without knowing what they were doing or why they were doing it, the depressed people reported that they were feeling much happier.

**Just the process of looking up and out
has the power to change everything.
When times are tough,
get out and look to the sky.**

Look at the sky. We are not alone. The whole universe is friendly to us and conspires only to give the best to those who dream and work.

A. P. J. Abdul Kalam

Key No.50: Use The "F" Word!

We've both worked with many people who were laden down with anger, resentment and the desire for revenge. Whenever we suggest that it might be better for their health and their future to forgive, the look on their faces is either one of horror or disgust! People will actually flinch and cringe when they hear the word 'forgiveness'. They really do seem to regard it as the other "F" word.

The main reason why people don't want to forgive is because they think that forgiveness means that they condone what happened to them. It's particularly apparent in those who have suffered mental, emotional or physical abuse. But that's not how we see forgiveness. We see it as the route to freeing yourself.

It's not about the person who hurt you or took advantage of you; you can't do anything about them or what goes on in their heads. What you can do is look after yourself and liberate yourself from the prison of your anger or resentment.

As a wise person once said, "Holding a grudge is like drinking poison and expecting the other person to die."

There are huge emotional costs in allowing someone to have power over how you feel, particularly if it's a long time after the actual event. Resentment is like rising damp; easy enough to paint over and hide temporarily, but until it's treated properly, it'll keep spreading. Don't paint over your problems! Forgiveness can be an incredibly powerful choice. Let it get rid of the anger that makes your life unhealthy.

Bonus Key: Find Your True Essence

In 1957, a group of monks in Thailand had to relocate their temple to a new location. Their sacred Buddha statue was 10 feet tall and made of clay. While it was being moved, it had to be stored outside overnight. The head monk decided to cover the Buddha with a large canvas to protect it. Later that evening, he went to check on the statue, shining his torch under the canvas to see if the Buddha was still dry. He noticed a glean catch the light and wondered whether there might be something under the clay. Using a chisel and hammer, he started to chip it away. As he knocked off shards of clay, the glean grew brighter and brighter.

The monk discovered that under the clay was an extraordinary solid gold Buddha, who measured 10 feet tall and weighed over two and a half tonnes.

Experts believe that several hundred years earlier, when the Burmese army was about to invade Thailand, the monks of the time had covered their precious golden Buddha with a coating of clay to protect it.

We are all like the clay Buddha, covered with a protective shell of hardness created out of fear. Inside each of us is a golden Buddha, which is our real self. Somewhere along the way, between the ages of two and nine, we began to cover up the golden essence of our natural selves. Just like the monk with the hammer and chisel, your goal is to find your true essence once again.

Don't hide your light anymore. It's time to shine!

Conclusion

**"By making a personal commitment
to our own individual transformational process,
we automatically begin to transform
the world around us."**

Shakti Gawain, *The Path of Transformation*

You now have all the tools and secrets you need to stop the quacking of your internal voice and change your life! If you take one thing away from this book, let it be this - there is nothing wrong with you. Maybe you once thought that you weren't good enough, or didn't deserve happiness, but this isn't true. If that little negative voice ever speaks up again, then just tell it to "Shut the Duck Up!"

It doesn't matter what challenges you face throughout your life; what's important is the way in which you face them, and the meaning you attach to them. Please have the courage to make the most of your beautiful life. Soar like an eagle, don't quack like a duck.

We send you love and wish you luck in achieving all your goals and ambitions. We know you can do it!

Bobby and Pete

Tales of a Life Coach

Have you heard of the new social media application Periscope? It's a service owned by Twitter where you can receive LIVE broadcasts direct to your smartphone, from me to you as they happen.

I'll be sharing regular advice 100% FREE daily at 7am covering all areas of life coaching and personal development. If you miss the live broadcast, then not to worry, as you can watch the replay at anytime.

So if that sounds good to you, and you want regular tips, tools, motivation and strategies to a better life 100% FREE, get yourself ready by downloading the Periscope app now and follow me using the instructions below.

Call it my manifesto, call it what you like, but I want to use Periscope to help people create a better life for themselves. So if you feel your best days are ahead of you and you want to achieve more, be happier, and more successful, then tune in as I go live at 7am every day. If you miss the periscope, you can always catch up and see the replay here www.talesofalifecoach.com

Think of it as a valuable free resource, think of it as a top coach dispensing advice for nothing, think of it what you will, but it's there and I'm there to be exploited. All I want in return is for thousands of people to join in the conversation and share their positive tales too.

We all want to live a happy life and we all recognise there are constructive changes that can be made to improve things. We're all on a journey, so let's share it with the world and create a snowball effect of positivity!

Download the Periscope app to your phone or tablet, and dive into the experience – let's make a difference together.

1. Install Periscope on your smartphone. It's 100% FREE and can be found for both Apple and Android devices.
2. Open up the app and click the 'People' icon found on the far right.
3. Click the magnifying glass icon; this will allow you to search for people in Periscope.
4. Find me by typing 'petecohen' and click the '+' icon to follow me. Now you'll get live notifications every time we go live with a broadcast.

I can't wait to share with you. Look out for those notifications starting soon.

Periscope allows you to tell your tale. It allows you to share your journey with like-minded people, and I believe it has the power to make a difference.

All the best,

Pete Cohen

Mi365 is a live broadcast every weekday at 7 a.m (UK time) which is designed to help people make positive changes in their lives. Thousands of people tune in live, or watch the replay, to benefit from my free coaching.

Join me, Pete Cohen, and learn how I can help you to change your mindset and improve the way you live your life: https://mi365elite.me/free-group

Lightning Source UK Ltd.
Milton Keynes UK
UKOW06f2055190917
309506UK00004B/35/P